Helicopter Directory

Helicopter Directory

By Joseph Mill Brown

David & Charles · Newton Abbot · London · Vancouver
Hippocrene Books Inc · New York

ISBN Great Britain 0 7153 7053 7

Library of Congress Cataloging in Publication Data
Brown, Joseph Mill.
    Helicopter directory.
    1. Helicopters — Catalogs. I. Title.
TL716.B73   1976   629.133'35   75-44234
ISBN 0-88254-382-2

Set in 8D on 9pt Univers Light
and printed in Great Britain
by Redwood Burn, Trowbridge and Esher
for David & Charles (Publishers) Limited
Brunel House   Newton Abbot   Devon

Published in the United States by
Hippocrene Books, Inc.
171 Madison Avenue
New York, N.Y. 10016

Published in Canada
by Douglas David & Charles Limited
1875 Welch Street   North Vancouver   BC

Contents

Introduction

A riffle through these pages and it is soon evident that the United States remains the world's most prolific supplier of helicopters. The primary producer (especially if one considers its vast licensing structure) must be the Bell Helicopter Co, although significant passenger and military patterns will continue to emanate from Sikorsky, Boeing Vertol, Hughes and Kaman.

The greatest variety of rotor aircraft in western Europe reposes in the confines of Italy's Agusta complex. Apart from its considerable licensing agreements with Bell, its own developed models attest to a formidable future.

The Soviet Union's helicopters comprise some of the largest cargo transports in the world. The sophisticated weaponry and electronic gear of their military types are not less than might be expected from a superpower, but the passenger and executive transports shown herein display a degree of luxury more usually associated with the West.

The combine formed in the 1970s by Great Britain's Westland and France's Aerospatiale has preserved parity in both the military and commercial spheres with a varied range of successful helicopters, whereas West Germany's rotocraft programme centres primarily on the BO 105 of Messerschmitt-Bolkow-Blohm. Helicopters produced in most other countries are more often the result of licensing agreements, although current experimental activity (in Japan, Israel, Argentina) suggests independent programmes in the not distant future.

As a military aircraft, the helicopter may be said to have first come fully into its own in the Korean war, when production rose to average almost a thousand per year soon after it had become evident that VTOL aircraft were ideal for rescue of the wounded, and for reconnaissance duties.

In Vietnam, the helicopter's missions were expanded to include the transport of troops and heavy equipment and, as 'gunships', displayed a formidable combat capacity when armed with machine guns, rockets and missiles. But the war also pointed up the helicopter's limitations; especially its inability to project speed beyond the present 300mph maximum. (No matter how powerful the engine, the rotors—which effect the vertical take-off—set a limit to forward speed.)

The helicopter as the transport vehicle to pierce the maze of congested cities is also a far-from-imminent reality, the resistance here, as elsewhere, being generated by the public fear of possible accidents in crowded city areas. The brightest outlook for the helicopter today may stem from the wealth of activity spurred by the boom of offshore oil and natural gas explorations. In the outer reaches of the North Sea, Sikorsky 61s (for one example) have already proved themselves in supply, transport and evacuation duties, often in the face of violent storms and hurricane-force winds.

If and when the breakthrough of the 300mph barrier becomes a reality, the helicopter—with its new potential for heavy-lift transport and reconnaissance—seems destined to be aviation's chariot in the movement away from dependence as a largely military support vehicle to genuine leadership in diverse areas of commercial transport.

A book such as this owes its life to the kindnesses of many people. My gratitude to all of them. Especially do I want to thank Bart van der Klaauw, Editor-in-Chief of *Avia*, that excellent Dutch monthly aerospace journal; Messrs J. Schrier and J. W. Maas of the Royal Netherlands Aeronautical Association; Mr I. M. Crasnick, Contracting Officer for the United States Army's plant activity at Hughes Helicopters; and The Royal Aeronautical Society's library staff in London.

My wife (as usual) did most of the hard work.

Joseph Mill Brown/The Hague, 1975

Argentina Cicare Aeronautica CH III Colibri

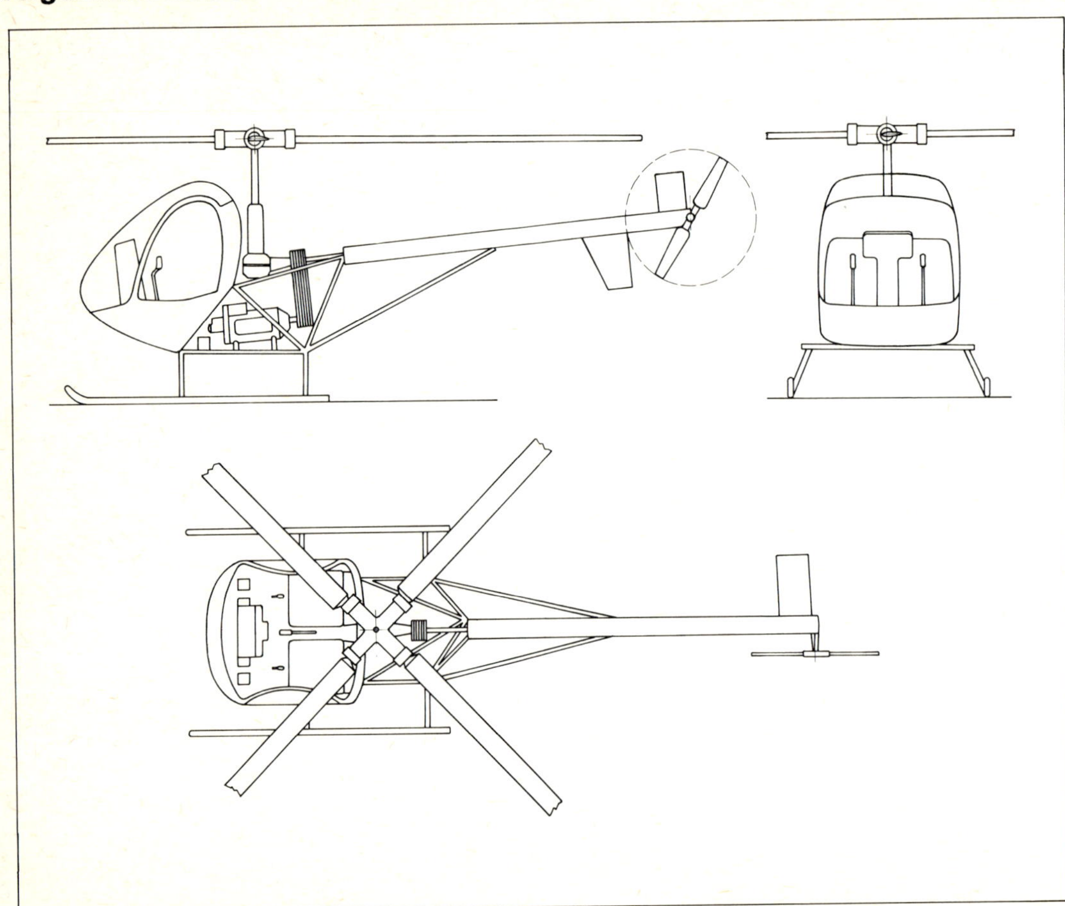

A prototype of the Colibri is being built by Cicare Aeronautica under agreement with the Argentine government.

The helicopter has a four-bladed main rotor of rigid configuration. The blades are of constant section and glassfibre construction. The tail rotor is two-bladed and of fibreglass.

The fuselage is of steel tube structure, with an aluminium tail boom and fibreglass cabin. The tail unit has horizontal and vertical fibreglass fixed stabilizers. The landing gear is a tubular skid type. The Colibri is being constructed for one/three-seat accommodation.

France Aerospatiale/SA 315B Lama

Engine
Turbomeca Artouste IIIB;
derated to 550shp
Rotor diameter
36ft 1¾in (11.02m)
Length overall
42ft 4¾in (12.92m)
Length of fuselage
33ft 8in (10.26m)
Weight empty
2,193lb (995kg)
Weight loaded
4,850lb (2,200kg)
Cruising speed
75mph (120km/h)
Rate of climb
820ft/m (250m)
Service ceiling
13,125ft (4,000m)
Hover ceiling OG
9,185ft (2,800m)

In 1972 the Lama set a world
altitude record of 40,810ft
(12,442m). Earlier, in the
Himalayas, it effected the only
helicopter landing at an elevation
of 24,600ft (7,500m), carrying
a crew of two with but one
hour's fuel on board.

Its mountain performance was
followed by a production
requirement for the armed forces
of India under the name of
Cheetah.

France Aerospatiale/SA 316B Alouette III

Engine
Turbomeca Artouste IIIB;
derated to 570shp
Rotor diameter
36ft 1¾in (11.02m)
Length overall
42ft 1½in (12.84m)
Weight empty
2,474lb (1,122kg)
Weight loaded
4,850lb (2,200kg)
Cruising speed
115mph (185km/h)
Rate of climb
885ft/m (270m)
Service ceiling
13,125ft (4,000m)
Hover ceiling IG
7,380ft (2,250m)
Range
335 miles (540km)

Developed from the Alouette II, with larger cabin capacity, greater power and improved equipment. In civilian and military use.

The three-bladed rotor system derived from the Alouette II, and the landing gear is non-retractable, with provision for a pontoon.

The military version includes 7.62mm machine-guns and can be equipped with wire-guided missiles. The naval version possesses a three-axis stabilisation system for activity against small surface craft and carries two homing torpedoes in the fuselage.

France Aerospatiale /SA 318C Alouette II Astazou

Engine
Turbomeca Astazou IIA;
derated to 360shp
Rotor diameter
33ft 5⅝in (10.20m)
Length overall
39ft 8½in (12.10m)
Length of fuselage
31ft 11¾in (9.75m)
Weight empty
1,961lb (890kg)
Weight loaded
3,630lb (1,650kg)
Cruising speed
112mph (180km/h)
Rate of climb
820ft/m (250m)
Service ceiling
10,800ft (3,300m)
Hover ceiling IGE*
5,085ft (1,550m)
Hover ceiling OGE**
2,950ft (900m)
Range
447 miles (720m)
(* in ground effect)
(** out of ground effect)

A light utility, light observation
helicopter that is adaptable for
use as a flying crane in
agricultural, photographic and
ambulance duties. Accommodates
a pilot and passenger up front;
three passengers behind. In
ambulance form there is room
for two stretchers and an
attendant.

France Aerospatiale/SA 319 Alouette III Astazou

Engine
Astazou XIV; derated to 600shp
Rotor diameter
36ft 1¾in (11.02m)
Length overall
42ft 1½in (12.84m)
Weight empty
2,442lb (1,108kg)
Weight loaded
4,960lb (2,250kg)
Cruising speed
122mph (197km/h)
Rate of climb
885ft/m (270m)
Hover ceiling IGE
7,380ft (2,250m)
Range
375 miles (605km)

Derived from the SA 316B. Its main departure is the possession of an Astazou XIV turboshaft engine, giving it a higher speed, greater range and lower fuel consumption than the 316B.

France Aerospatiale /SA 321 Super Frelon

Engines
Three (3) Turbomeca Turmo
IIIC6-70; 1,630shp
Rotor diameter
62ft 0in (18.90m)
Length overall
75ft 6⅝in (23.03m)
Length of fuselage
65ft 10¾in (20.08m)
Weight empty
15,873lb (7,200kg)
Weight loaded
28,660lb (13,000kg)
Cruising speed
155mph (249km/h)
Rate of climb
1,312ft/m (400m)
Service ceiling
10,325ft (3,150m)
Hover ceiling IGE
7,120ft (2,170m)
Range
633 miles (1,020km)

A three-engined multi-purpose helicopter produced under a cooperative agreement with Sikorsky of U.S.A. (design, construction, testing of rotor systems) and Fiat of Italy (production of main gearcase and transmission box).

The civilian version (SA 321F) carries up to thirty-seven passengers. Duties of the anti-submarine model (SA 321G) include support of nuclear submarines at French bases. The SA 321J is a public transport vehicle for personnel and cargo.

Six main rotor blades and a five-blade anti-torque tail rotor, all-metal and interchangeable, connect through to the turbine engines which surround the main gearbox. All versions are geared for all-weather performance.

Engines
Two (2) Turmo IV C ; 1,575shp
Rotor diameter
49ft 2½in (15.00m)
Length overall
59ft 6½in (18.15m)
Length of fuselage
46ft 1½in (14.06m)
Weight empty
7,403lb (3,358kg)
Weight loaded
14,770lb (6,700kg)
Cruising speed
162mph (261km/h)
Rate of climb
1,380ft/m (420m)
Hover ceiling IGE
6,890ft (2,100m)
Hover ceiling OGE
4,265ft (1,300m)
Range
385 miles (620km)

A twin-turbine tactical transport helicopter, produced jointly with Great Britain's Westland Helicopters Ltd, to meet a fifteen-year requirement schedule of the French and British armed forces.

Various categories include the 330B (for the French Army) ; the 330C (for military export) ; the 330E (for the Royal Air Force ; designated Puma HC Mk 1), and the 330F (civilian passengers and cargo).

Hydraulically-actuated systems can be operated on the ground from the main gearbox. An auxiliary system, manipulated via a handpump, is available in an emergency for settling the landing gear and parking device.

Specialised electronics equipment complement a variety of armaments including 20mm cannon, 7.62mm machine-guns, and missiles.

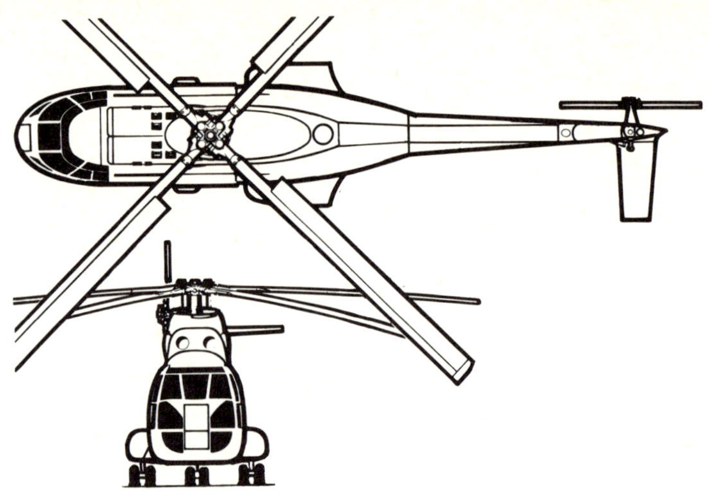

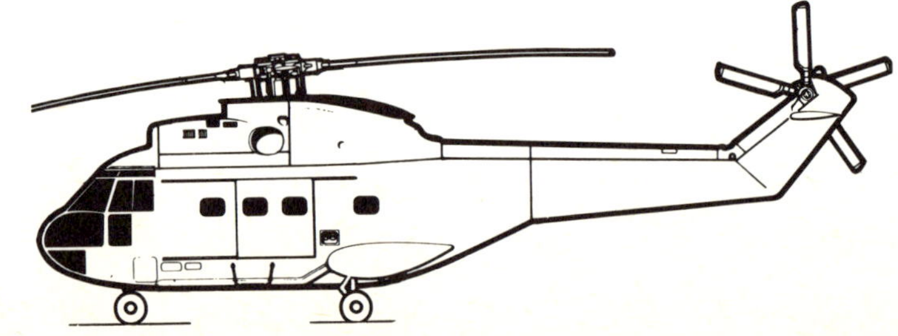

F-ZWWN
SA330

Engine
Turbomeca Astazou III ; 590shp
Rotor diameter
34ft 5½in (10.50m)
Length overall
39ft 3⁵⁄₁₆in (11.97m)
Length of fuselage
31ft 3³⁄₁₆in (9.53m)
Weight empty
2,002lb (908kg)
Weight loaded
3,970lb (1,800kg)
Cruising speed
164mph (264km/h)
Rate of climb
1,770ft/m (540m)
Service ceiling
16,400ft (5,000m)
Hover ceiling IGE
9,350ft (2,850m)
Hover ceiling OGE
6,560ft (2,000m)
Range
416 miles (670km)

A light utility helicopter of advanced design, produced jointly with Britain's Westland Helicopters Ltd, for military and civil use. World speed records were set in 1971, topped by a 312km/h mark over a straight course.

The Gazelle's design features five fold-away seats for interchangeability, a semi-articulated rotor with laminated fibreglass blades, and a shrouded 'fenestron' tail rotor for ground safety. (The 'fenestron' is set into a vertical fin in contrast to the exposed tail rotor position.)

Rotor system provides for a three-blade main rotor and thirteen-blade tail rotor. Main gearbox is mounted above rear of the cabin. Blind-flying instrumentation is standard on the British and French army version ; optional on all others. Military equipment can provide sight systems, including four TOW missiles.

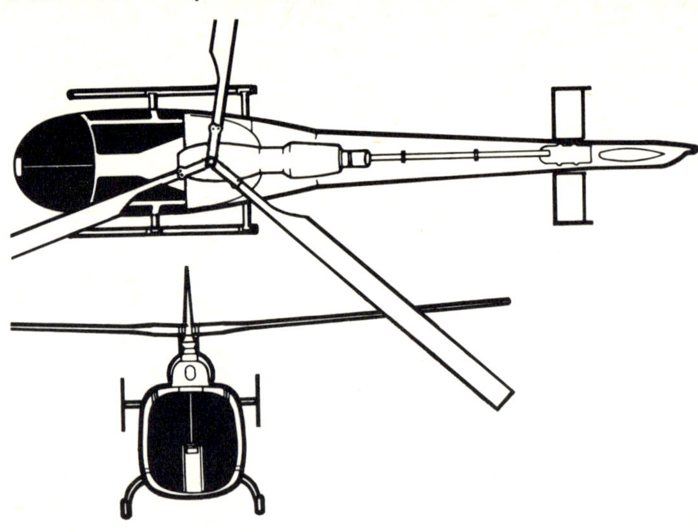

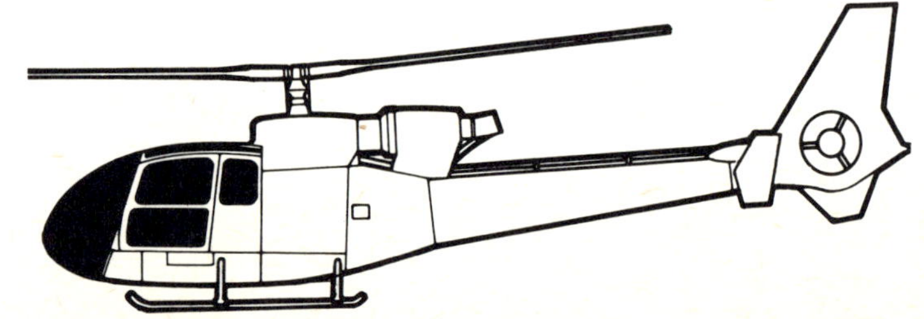

Engine
Turbomeca Astazou XVIA ;
980shp
Rotor diameter
37ft 8¾in (11.50m)
Length overall
44ft 0in (13.41m)
Length of fuselage
36ft 3⅞in (11.07m)
Weight empty
3,087lb (1,400kg)
Weight loaded
5,953lb (2,700kg)
Cruising speed
171mph (275km/h)
Hover ceiling IGE
10,500ft (3,200m)
Hover ceiling OGE
9,200ft (2,800m)
Range
372 miles (600km)

A turbine-powered all-purpose
helicopter intended as a follow-
up to the Alouette III.
Expected to be on the market
in 1976.
Like the Gazelle, the SA 360
has a 'fenestron' type tail rotor.
Its seating capacity is ten (pilot
and nine passengers). Can be
converted to rescue and cargo
work.

Engine
Turbomeca Astazou II ; 500hp
Rotor diameter
30ft 10in (9.40m)
Rotor blade chord
$9\frac{1}{4}$in (0.235m)
Weight empty
992lb (450kg)
Weight loaded
2,336lb (1,060kg)
Maximum speed
124mph (200km/h)
Range

372 miles (600km)
First exhibited at the 1969 Paris Air Show, this light helicopter (constructed by owner Charles Dechaux) has a four-bladed main rotor. The cabin is of light alloy and two booms support the tail unit. The Helicop-Jet seats four people in side-by-side pairs.

Engines
Two Rolls-Royce Continental
TSIO-360-A; 210hp, or two
T6-320 Tiara; 320hp
Rotor diameter
33ft 0in (10.06m)
Length overall
36ft 2in (11.02m)
Length of fuselage
28ft 2in (8.58m)
Weight empty
2,212lb (1,003kg)
Weight loaded
3,450lb (1,564kg)
Cruising speed
127mph (204km/h)
Rate of climb
1,300ft/m (396m)
Service ceiling
20,000ft (6,100m)
Hover ceiling OGE
9,500ft (2,895m)
Range
449 miles (722km)

Cierva Rotorcraft Ltd was
formed to develop rotorcraft
embodying the principles first
established in 1926 by the
Spanish inventor of the
autogiro, Juan de la Cierva,
and since by his successors.

The CR Twin is a light utility
helicopter. Its co-axial, contra-
rotating rotor system maintains
balance without requiring a tail
rotor. The tail unit has a single
fin and rudder. The two blades

of the rotor system are of
plastics, tapered, and attached
to the hubs by hinges. Blades
are not foldable. The
electrical system provides for
two 12V 60A alternators.

There is side-by-side seating
in front for pilot and co-pilot
or passenger, and space for
three more passengers in the
rear.

Engine
Two (2) Rolls-Royce Gnome H
1400 ; 1,500shp
Rotor diameter
62ft 0in (18.90m)
Length overall
72ft 8in (22.15m)
Length of fuselage
55ft 9¾in (17.01m)
Weight empty
13,181lb (5,978kg)
Weight loaded
20,500lb (9,300kg)
Cruising speed
131mph (211km/h)
Rate of climb
1,770ft/m (540m)
Service ceiling
10,000ft (3,050m)
Range
863 miles (1,390km)

Westland Aircraft's entry into the helicopter field began with a licensing agreement, in 1947, to produce the Sikorsky S-51. Its main impact is now in the helicopter field; and its co-production agreement with Aerospatiale of France has established the group as among the most formidable suppliers in the western world.

The Sea King is a Westland answer to the Royal Navy's requirement for a durable anti-submarine weapon (ASW) and a search-and-rescue (SAR)

vehicle. It is fitted with an automatic flight control system, and doppler and search radars. (Sonar is carried on the anti-submarine version.)

The ASW version carries a crew of four (two pilots, a control officer, and sonar operator). The SAR will accommodate up to twenty-two passengers.

Cargo is expedited via a personnel door on the port side and a freight door to starboard.

A hoist (272kg capacity) is situated above the starboard door, and a freight sling can be fitted to carry loads externally, up to 3,630kg.

Engines
Two (2) Rolls-Royce Gnome H,
1400-1 ; 1,590shp
Rotor diameter
62ft 0in (18.90m)
Length overall
72ft 8in (22.15m)
Length of fuselage
55ft 10in (17.02m)
Weight empty
11,487lb (5,210kg)
Weight loaded
21,000lb (9,525kg)
Cruising speed
129mph (208km/h)
Rate of climb
2,013ft/m (614m)
Service ceiling
4,000ft (1,220m)
Hover ceiling IGE
5,000ft (1,525m)
Hover ceiling OGE
3,200ft (975m)
Range
967 miles (1,556km)

The Westland Commando is designed as an army logistic support aircraft and is a development of the same company's Sea King. Its more powerful Rolls-Royce Gnome engines give 135shp more per engine. The main rotor gearbox has been up-rated to 2,700shp.

The helicopter has a five-bladed main rotor and a six-bladed tail rotor. The fuel system has a 3,714 litre capacity. An auxiliary fuel tank, which can be stored in the main cabin, has a maximum capacity of 680kg (1,502lb).

Seats are provided for a crew of two and twenty-seven troops.

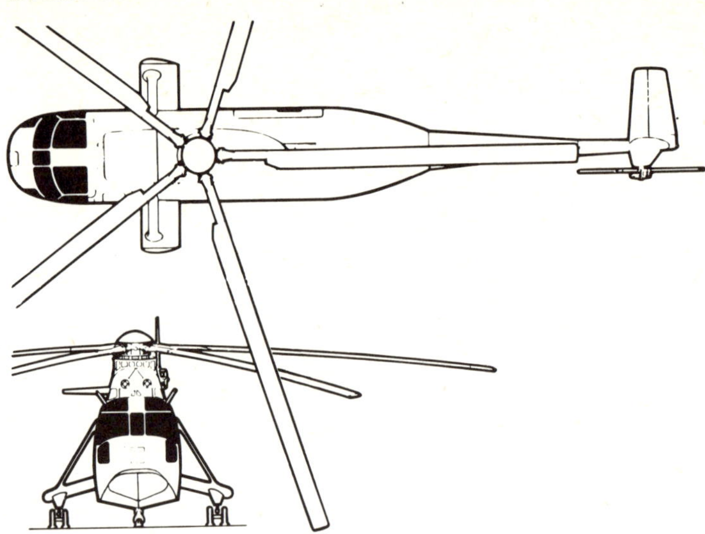

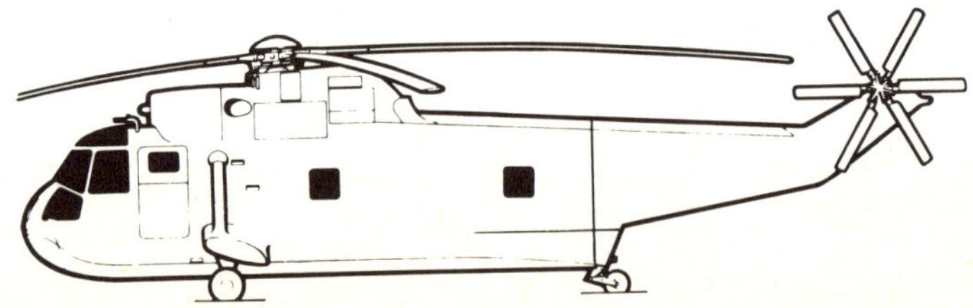

Great Britain Westland /WA Lynx AH Mk 1

Engines
Two (2) Rolls-Royce BS
360-07-26 ; 750shp
Rotor diameter
42ft 0in (12.80m)
Length overall
49ft 9in (15.16m)
Length of fuselage
39ft 0¾in (12.06m)
Weight empty
5,216lb (2,366kg)
Weight loaded
8,250lb (3,742kg)
Cruising speed
184mph (296km/h)
Rate of climb
2,800ft/m (853m)
Hover ceiling OGE
12,000ft (3,650m)

The Lynx is the latest
collaborative effort between
Westland and Aerospatiale
for a multi-purpose army, navy
and civil helicopter, and is
planned for service in 1975.

It has a semi-rigid rotor head ;
two of the usual three hinges
are of flap-and-lag titanium
elements. Manifold units are
utilised for each of the two main
hydraulic systems in order to
group their components in an
accessible area. A wide variety
of armaments and avionics are
standard. The army version of
the Lynx can be fitted with
flotation gear for search-and-
rescue missions.

In 1972, the Army Lynx set
two world class speed records
of 200mph (321.4km/h).

Great Britain Westland /WA Lynx HAS Mk 2

Engines
Two (2) Rolls-Royce BS
360-07-26 ; 750shp
Rotor diameter
42ft 0in (12.80m)
Length overall
49ft 9in (15.16m)
Length of fuselage
39ft ⅓in (11.92m)
Weight empty
5,546lb (2,515kg)
Weight loaded
9,250lb (4,195kg)
Cruising speed
170mph (270km/h)
Range
472 miles (754km)

The Navy version of the Lynx has a tricycle undercarriage and a harpoon deck lock securing system for small-craft operation in all-weather conditions. Its anti-submarine mission craft can be armed with two homing torpedoes or two depth charges and six marine markers. The anti-shipping, search-and-strike unit employs search radar, a lightweight sighting system, and four wire-guided missiles.

As a troop transport, the Navy Lynx can accommodate a commander and nine troops; as an ambulance, conversion can provide room for three stretchers, plus a medical attendant. An underslung cargo of 2,992lb (1,360kg) can be carried.

Great Britain Westland /Wasp

Engine
Rolls-Royce Bristol Nimbus
503; derated to 710shp
Rotor diameter
32ft 3in (9.83m)
Length overall
40ft 4in (12.29m)
Length of fuselage
30ft 4in (9.24m)
Weight empty
3,452lb (1,566kg)
Weight loaded
5,500lb (2,495kg)
Cruising speed
110mph (177km/h)
Rate of climb
1,440ft/m (439m)
Service ceiling
12,200ft (3,720m)
Hover ceiling IGE
12,500ft (3,810m)
Hover ceiling OGE
8,800ft (2,682m)
Range
270 miles (435km)

A development for the Royal
Navy as an all-weather, anti-
submarine helicopter. It has
foldable main rotor blades to
facilitate shipboard storage, a
torsion-bar blade-suspension
device, a four-blade main rotor
and two-blade tail rotor.

The landing gear is non-
retractable and the four wheels
recline on shock-absorber
struts. Equipment includes

standard blind-flying instruments
and an autostabilisation system
with radio altimeter. There are
two side-by-side seats at the
front of the cabin and a bench
for three spaces at the rear,
which can be removed for cargo
substitution.

The Wasp is in service with
the navies of Brazil, New
Zealand, South Africa and the
Netherlands, which gave the
helicopter the designation
AH-12A.

Great Britain Westland/Wessex HC Mk 2

Engine
Two (2) Bristol Siddeley
Gnome H 1200; 1,350shp
Rotor diameter
56ft (17.07m)
Length of fuselage
49ft 11in (15.21m)
Weight empty
7,850lb (3,560kg)
Weight loaded
13,500lb (6,123kg)
Cruising speed
126mph (203km/h)
Rate of climb
1,700ft/m (518m)
Service ceiling
10,000ft (3,048m)
Range
310 miles (499km)

The Wessex developed from a Royal Navy requirement in the 1950s for a general naval helicopter. Its original basis was a Sikorsky S-58 helicopter fitted with Napier-Gazelle engines. Eventually the Wessex was produced for various functions, military and civil, and acquired along the way Rolls-Royce and Bristol Siddeley Gnome power plants. In its variants it has served as a commando carrier for the Royal Navy, a troop transport for the Royal Air Force, and has been supplied to the air forces of Iraq and Ghana. The civil version (Wessex 60) has been active since the mid-1960s in the oil and natural gas explorations conducted in the North Sea.

Italy Agusta /47G-3B-2

Engine
Lycoming TVO-435-G1A;
280hp
Rotor diameter
37ft 1⅛in (11.31m)
Length overall
43ft 2½in (13.17m)
Length of fuselage
32ft 6in (9.90m)
Weight empty
1,937lb (878kg)
Weight loaded
2,950lb (1,338kg)
Cruising speed
83mph (133km/h)
Rate of climb
990ft/m (302m)
Service ceiling
18,400ft (5,608m)
Hover ceiling IGE
16,600ft (5,060m)
Hover ceiling OGE
12,300ft (3,750m)
Range
250 miles (402km)

A commercial version of the American Bell Model 107, the 47G-3B-2 is a high-altitude helicopter. It has a high inertia main rotor, with hydraulic servo-control of cyclic and collective pitch. Interval between overhauls is stated to be 1,200 hours.

The 47G-3B-2 can provide accommodation for a pilot and two passengers or, alternatively two litters fitted in outside holders. It is used by the Italian police, army and air force.

Engine
Lycoming TVO-435-B1A;
rated at 270hp
Rotor diameter
37ft 1½in (11.32m)
Length overall
43ft 7½in (13.30m)
Length of fuselage
31ft 7in (9.63m)
Weight empty
1,863lb (845kg)
Weight loaded
2,950lb (1,340kg)
Cruising speed
86mph (138km/h)
Rate of climb
905ft/m (276m)
Service ceiling
17,500ft (5,340m)
Hover ceiling IGE
16,500ft (5,030m)
Hover ceiling OGE
12,200ft (3,720m)
Range
210 miles (338km)

A high-altitude helicopter with four-seat accommodation, manufactured under licence from the Bell Helicopter Corporation.

The 47J-3B-1 is easily adapted for light transport and evacuation services in mountainous regions by the fitting of supplemental installations, such as cabin litters and snow skids. It is in service with the Italian army, air force and police.

The helicopter has a high-inertia main rotor with cyclic and hydraulic servo-control systems. The Lycoming engine is fitted with a turbo-supercharger for preserving sea-level conditions at ceiling heights.

Engine
Pratt & Whitney S1H4
(R-1340) ; 600hp
Rotor diameter
47ft 6¾in (14.50m)
Length overall
41ft 9¼in (12.73m)
Weight empty
3,990lb (1,814kg)
Weight loaded
6,660lb (3,027kg)
Cruising speed
100mph (160km/h)
Rate of climb
1,100ft/m (336m)
Service ceiling
12,800ft (3,904m)
Hover ceiling IGE
8,100ft (2,471m)
Range
248 miles (394km)

Based on the American Bell
Model 48, the 102 was re-
designed as a utility helicopter
for the transport of passengers
and freight. Converted for
ambulance duties, it can
accommodate four stretcher
cases.

Italy Agusta /A 106

Engine
Turbomeca-Agusta TAA 230;
derated to 330shp
Rotor diameter
31ft 2in (9.50m)
Length overall
36ft 0in (10.975m)
Length of fuselage
28ft 6½in (8.70m)
Weight empty
1,300lb (590kg)
Weight loaded
3,086lb (1,400kg)
Cruising speed
105mph (169km/h)
Rate of climb
1,230ft/m (375m)
Hover ceiling IGE
8,350ft (2,545m)
Hover ceiling OGE
3,700ft (1,127m)
Range
460 miles (740km)

This single-seat helicopter is being produced by Agusta specifically for anti-submarine duty. It carries two Mk 44 torpedoes, and is equipped with inflatable pontoons, an external cargo hook, and a Ferranti three-axis stability augmentation system. Its fuel capacity can reach 132 imperial gallons (600 litres).

Italy Agusta/A 109 Hirundo

Engines
Two (2) Allison 250-C20;
400shp
Rotor diameter
36ft 1in (11.00m)
Length of fuselage
36ft ¾in (10.99m)
Weight empty
2,645lb (1,200kg)
Weight loaded
5,070lb (2,300kg)
Cruising speed
138mph (220km/h)
Rate of climb
2,060ft/m (630m)
Service ceiling
17,400ft (5,300m)
Hover ceiling IGE
11,810ft (3,600m)
Hover ceiling OGE
9,190ft (2,800m)
Range
457 miles (735km)

This twin-engined helicopter accommodates a pilot and seven passengers in a civil transport capacity which can be modified for cargo and rescue work. The cargo hook is located at the centre of gravity of the helicopter; an external rescue hoist with a cable length of 100ft (30m) is capable of raising up to 375lb (170kg).

The tricycle-type landing gear can be retracked by means of an electro-hydraulic system. The rotor system comprises a four-bladed main and a two-bladed tail of semi-rigid, bonded metal type. The main rotor blades may be manually folded to facilitate parking in crowded areas.

Italy Agusta /A 120B Helibus

Engines
Three (3) General Electric
T64-GE-12 ; 3,500hp
Rotor diameter
72ft 2in (22.00m)
Length overall
85ft 11½in (26.20m)
Weight empty
31,306lb (14,200kg)
Weight loaded
51,809lb (23,500kg)
Cruising speed
250mph (400km/h)
Service ceiling
20,000ft (6,100m)
Hover ceiling IGE
10,000ft (3,100m)
Hover ceiling OGE
6,000ft (1,800m)
Range
335 miles (700km)

This helicopter is under development as a high-speed 'compound' craft suitable for the transport of passengers and goods over medium distances (375-450 miles ; 600-700km).

Two engines are located in wing nacelles and power the main drive, each engine driving one tractor propeller through a special gearbox. The propellers are controlled directly to reverse pitch, and on control are synchronised with the main rotor. The third engine is located inside the fuselage and drives the main transmission.

The A 120B Helibus takes four crew and sixty-five

Italy Agusta /A 129

Engines
Two (2) Allison 250-C20;
400shp
Rotor diameter
36ft 1in (11.00m)
Length of fuselage
36ft ¾in (10.99m)
Weight loaded
5,720lb (2,600kg)
Maximum speed
200mph (320km/h)
Hover ceiling OGE
8,100ft (2,500m)
Range
480 miles (768km)

The A 129 is under development
by Agusta as an anti-tank
helicopter. The company has
employed basic components of
its A 109 Hirundo, and fitted
the A 129 with an armament
system that includes TOW
missiles. The helicopter is
planned to be equipped with
free rockets and a ventral 7.62
minigun adjustable over 360°
in horizontal plane, and 80°
Minitat system in the vertical
plane.

Italy Agusta/AB 204AS

Engine
General Electric T58-GE-3;
1,290shp
Rotor diameter
48ft 0in (14.63m)
Length overall
57ft 0in (17.37m)
Length of fuselage
41ft 7in (12.67m)
Weight empty
6,481lb (2,940kg)
Weight loaded
9,501lb (4,310kg)
Cruising speed
104mph (167km/h)

This model, currently in service with the Italian and Spanish navies, is an anti-submarine version of the 204B which, in turn, has been sold to the armed forces and commercial concerns of a dozen countries in western Europe and the Middle East.

The 204AS is fitted for all-weather flights and equipped with sonar, radar and two Mk 44 torpedoes for action against small surface craft.

Its fuel load is 155 imperial gallons (705 litres).

Italy Agusta/AB 204B

Engine
Lycoming T53-11A; 1,100shp
Rotor diameter
48ft 0in (14.63m)
Weight empty
4,600lb (2,090kg)
Weight loaded
9,500lb (4,310kg)
Cruising speed
110mph (177km/h)
Rate of climb
1,400ft/m (427m)
Hover ceiling IGE
10,000ft (3,050m)
Hover ceiling OGE
4,500ft (1,370m)
Range
392 miles (630km)

A medium-size utility helicopter, based on the Bell Iroquois, the 204B has been fitted with main rotors of various sizes and diverse engines (Lycoming in this model), including Rolls-Royce, Bristol, Gnome and General Electric T58 turbo-shafts. Fuji, of Japan, produces the 204B with a Kawasaki-built engine.

Some of the countries which have purchased the 204B for their armed forces are Italy, Spain, Holland and Turkey. Civil versions have been sold to private concerns in Sweden and Switzerland.

Italy Agusta /AB 205

Engine
Lycoming T53-L-13; 1,400shp
Rotor diameter
48ft 0in (14.63m)
Length of fuselage
41ft 11in (12.78m)
Weight empty
4,800lb (2,177kg)
Weight loaded
9,500lb (4,310kg)
Cruising speed
132mph (212km/h)
Rate of climb
1,800ft/m (548m)
Hover ceiling IGE
17,000ft (5,180m)
Hover ceiling OGE
11,000ft (3,350m)
Range
360 miles (580km)

A further evolution of the Bell Helicopter UH-1 series, the 205 is operational with armed forces in many western countries. It has a capacity for fifteen troop seats and is fitted with instrument-flight rules and night-flying equipment. Its cargo capacity is 220cuft (6.2m³).

The 205 has a single-point cargo suspension hook (situated under the transmission) which can lift cargo bulks weighing up to 4,000lb (1,800kg). It can also be fitted with an electrical rescue hoist, mounted outside, with an external arm for immediate operation. The hoist has a 100ft (30m) cable capable of lifting up to 600lb (272kg).

Italy Agusta/AB 205A-1

Engine
Lycoming T53-L-13A; derated
to 1,250shp
Rotor diameter
48ft 0in (14.63m)
Length of fuselage
41ft 11in (12.78m)
Weight empty
5,195lb (2,356kg)
Weight loaded
10,500lb (4,762kg)
Cruising speed
126mph (203km/h)
Rate of climb
2,030ft/m (619m)
Hover ceiling IGE
11,000ft (3,350m)
Hover ceiling OGE
6,800ft (2,075m)
Range
331 miles (532km)

This is a civilian version of the
205 which Agusta put into
production in 1969. Its
passenger seats number
fourteen; baggage space totals
28.3cuft (0.8m³).

The 205A-1 may be fitted
with a variety of auxiliary
installations, including
amphibious landing gear,
flotation kits and snow skid
fittings, ambulance litters and
special cabin interiors for VIP
use.

Italy Agusta/AB 206A JetRanger

Engine
Allison 250-C18; 317shp
Rotor diameter
33ft 4in (10.16m)
Length overall
39ft 2in (11.94m)
Length of fuselage
31ft 2in (9.50m)
Weight empty
1,431lb (649kg)
Weight loaded
3,000lb (1,360kg)
Cruising speed
130mph (209km/h)
Rate of climb
1,450ft/m (442m)
Hover ceiling IGE
9,100ft (2,770m)
Hover ceiling OGE
3,500ft (1,065m)
Range
391 miles (629km)

A modification of the Bell
JetRanger, in production by
Agusta since 1966–7. The 206A
is a five-seat turbine-powered
helicopter, modified for civilian
and military use. Its conversions
have included executive
transport and amphibious
surveillance craft.

Italy Agusta/AB 206A-1

Engine
Allison 250-C18
Rotor diameter
35ft 4in (10.77m)
Length overall
41ft 0in (12.50m)
Length of fuselage
32ft 4in (9.85m)
Weight empty
1,504lb (682kg)
Weight loaded
3,000lb (1,360kg)
Cruising speed
127mph (204km/h)
Rate of climb
1,560ft/m (475m)
Hover ceiling IGE
10,900ft (3,325m)
Hover ceiling OGE
6,000ft (1,825m)
Range
368 miles (592km)

Agusta's counterpart to Bell's military OH-58A Kiowa, the 206A-1 (as with the B-1) has a larger rotor diameter, extra doors and mounts diverse weapons. Its endurance, based on standard fuel, is approximately four hours.

Italy Agusta/AB 206B JetRanger

Engine
Allison 250-C20; 400shp
Rotor diameter
33ft 4in (10.16m)
Length overall
38ft 9½in (11.82m)
Length of fuselage
31ft 2in (9.50m)
Weight empty
1,485lb (675kg)
Weight loaded
3,000lb (1,365kg)
Cruising speed
136mph (215km/h)
Service ceiling
20,000ft (6,095m)
Hover ceiling IGE
13,000ft (3,965m)
Hover ceiling OGE
10,000ft (3,050m)
Range
356 miles (604km)

A turbine-powered, five-place light helicopter which is operational in military and civil capacities in many countries of the world. In standard configuration, it is fully-equipped and ready to fly VFR, day or night. Navigation lights, landing and instrument lights, and anti-collision strobe are standard equipment, as are sound-proofing, fire extinguisher, first-aid kit and five seat belts.

A military version of the AB 206B, designed for the Italian Army, is comparable to the Bell's OH-58 'Kiowa' for the US Army.

Italy Agusta /AB 206B JetRanger II

Engine
Allison 250-C20; derated to
317shp
Rotor diameter
33ft 4in (10.16m)
Length overall
39ft 2in (11.94m)
Length of fuselage
31ft 2in (9.50m)
Weight empty
1,504lb (682kg)
Weight loaded
3,200lb (1,452kg)
Cruising speed
133mph (214km/h)
Rate of climb
1,358ft/m (414m)
Hover ceiling IGE
11,325ft (3,450m)
Hover ceiling OGE
5,800ft (1,770m)
Range
418 miles (673km)

A development of the 206A
JetRanger, which has now
become the Agusta standard.
Fully equipped for night flying,
the 206B features navigation
lights, landing lights, anti-
collision strobe, and instrument
lights.

The cabin has seats for pilot
and four passengers. Baggage
capacity is 250lb (113kg).

Italy Agusta /AB 206B-1

Engine
Allison 250-C20
Rotor diameter
35ft 4in (10.77m)
Length overall
41ft 0in (12.50m)
Length of fuselage
32ft 4in (9.85m)
Weight empty
1,540lb (698kg)
Weight loaded
3,200lb (1,452kg)
Cruising speed
129mph (208km/h)
Rate of climb
1,300ft/m (396m)
Hover ceiling IGE
12,000ft (3,660m)
Hover ceiling OGE
8,000ft (2,440m)
Range
334 miles (538km)

The 206B-1, which was put
into production in 1972,
provides accommodation for
pilot and four passengers.
Primary difference between this
and other 206B models consists
of diverse modifications for the
Italian armed forces and foreign
military customers.

Italy Agusta/AB 212

Engines
Two (2) Pratt & Whitney
UACL PT6T-3 Turbo Twin Pac;
1,800hp
Rotor diameter
48ft 0in (14.63m)
Length overall
57ft 1in (17.40m)
Length of fuselage
46ft 0in (14.02m)
Weight empty
5,800lb (2,630kg)
Weight loaded
11,200lb (5,081kg)
Cruising speed
127mph (204km/h)
Rate of climb
1,860ft/m (564m)
Service ceiling
17,000ft (5,180m)
Hover ceiling IGE
13,000ft (3,960m)
Hover ceiling OGE
10,000ft (3,050m)
Range
366 miles (589km)

This utility helicopter, primarily intended for civil transport, can accommodate a pilot and fourteen passengers. It is the first in its medium-weight class to be certified for instrument-flight rules. An automatic flight control system is available, which is hydraulically boosted, and all control systems are independently duplicated.

In ambulance form, the 212 can be adapted to carry six stretcher cases and two medical attendants. Optional extras include a rescue hoist, hook, flotation gear and auxiliary fuel tanks.

Italy Agusta /AS HH-3F

Engines
Two (2) General Electric
T58-GE-5 ; 1,500shp
Rotor diameter
62ft 0in (18.90m)
Length overall
73ft 0in (22.25m)
Length of fuselage
57ft 3in (17.45m)
Weight empty
11,688lb (5,294kg)
Weight loaded
22,050lb (9,988kg)
Cruising speed
123mph (228km/h)
Rate of climb
1,210ft/m (369m)
Service ceiling
13,600ft (4,145m)
Hover ceiling IGE
9,700ft (2,960m)
Range
470 miles (760km)

Designed as a vehicle for sea-
rescue and amphibious cargo
transport work, the HH-3F is a
twin turbine-engined helicopter
equipped with a variety of
sophisticated electronic systems
and cargo-moving equipment.

The rear ramp can be lowered
to platform position on the
surface of water to facilitate
embarkation of shipwrecked
passengers. On land, the same
rear ramp is used for loading
and unloading.

Standard configuration
provides seating for six
passengers, but can be enlarged
to accommodate twenty-five.

The hospital version can take
fifteen stretchers; alternatively,
four stretcher cases and ten
ambulatory patients.

Engine
Lycoming VO-540-B1B3;
derated to 250hp
Rotor diameter
31ft 2in (9.50m)
Weight empty
1,543lb (700kg)
Weight loaded
2,535lb (1,150kg)
Cruising speed
90mph (145km/h)
Rate of climb
827ft/m (252m)
Service ceiling
14,100ft (4,300m)
Hover ceiling IGE
8,200ft (2,500m)
Hover ceiling OGE
5,575ft (1,700m)
Range
260 miles (420km)

Meridionali was organised in
1967 with the assistance of
Agusta to overhaul helicopters
of the Italian military services.
The following year it was
granted co-production and
marketing rights for the Boeing
Vertol Ch-47C Chinook in
central Europe and the Middle
East.

In 1970, the company
produced and flew the EMA
124, a three-seat helicopter
designed by Agusta and derived
from the Bell Model 47. Its
main rotor has foldable twin

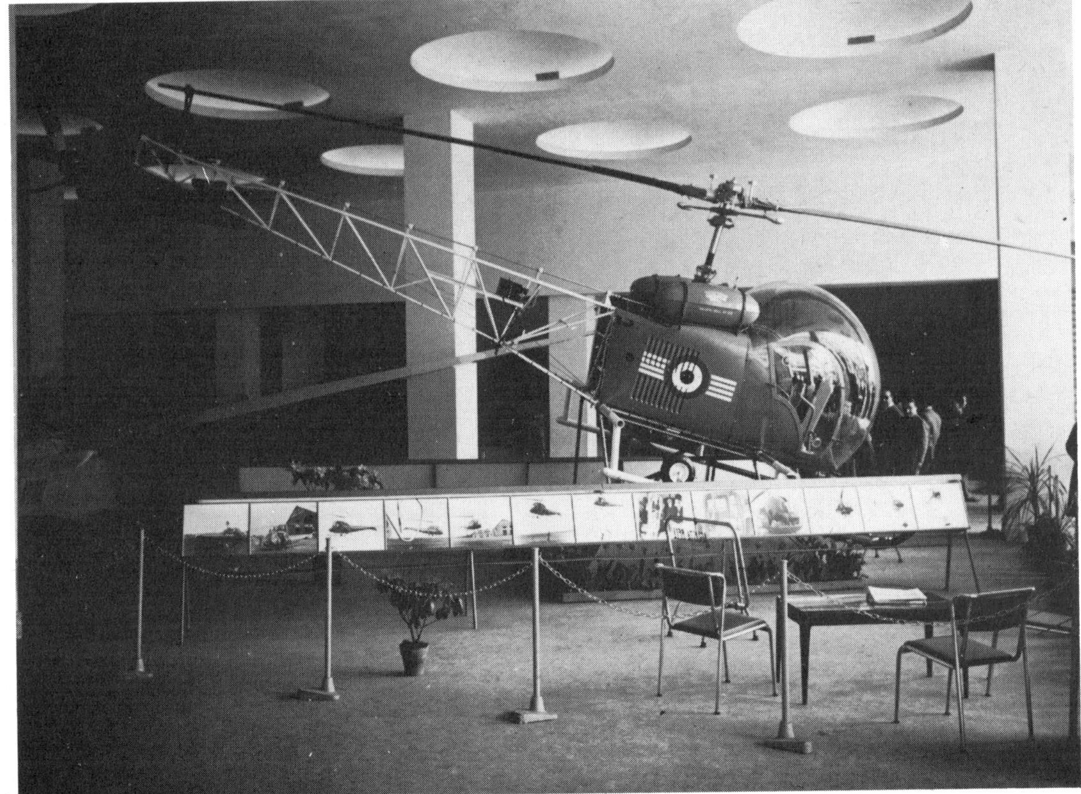

blades of semi-rigid con-
struction, as has the tail rotor.
The servo-control cylinders are
powered by a single hydraulic
system. Side-by-side seating is
provided for a pilot and two
passengers in an enclosed,
transparent cabin, with a
provision for dual controls.

Italy SIAI-Marchetti /SV-20A

Engines
Two (2) Pratt & Whitney
PT6C-30; 900shp
Rotor diameter
42ft 2½in (12.86m)
Length overall
51ft 3¼in (15.63m)
Length of fuselage
44ft 6¼in (13.57m)
Weight empty
5,445lb (2,470kg)
Weight loaded
10,400lb (4,717kg)
Cruising speed
202mph (325km/h)
Rate of climb
1,900ft/m (579m)
Hover ceiling IGE
20,000ft (6,100m)
Hover ceiling OGE
14,105ft (4,300m)
Range
403 miles (650km)

Founded in 1915, Siai-Marchetti has been a versatile manufacturer of conventional aircraft, passenger and freight cars, until little more than a decade ago when it embarked on a rotorcraft programme.

The SV-20A is a high-speed helicopter destined for commercial use in the late 1970s and can accommodate a pilot and twelve passengers, or equivalent cargo loads. The tail unit and landing gear are of aluminium alloy; the wings are cantilevered.

Fuel capacity totals 220 imperial gallons (1,000 litres), and oil capacity is 2 1/5 imperial gallons (10 litres).

Italy Silvercraft /SH-4

Engine
Franklin 6A-350-D1B; derated
to 170hp
Rotor diameter
29ft 7½in (9.03m)
Length overall
34ft 4¼in (10.47m)
Length of fuselage
25ft 1¼in (7.65m)
Weight empty
1,142lb (518kg)
Weight loaded
1,900lb (862kg)
Cruising speed
81mph (130km/h)
Rate of climb
1,180ft/m (360m)
Service ceiling
15,090ft (4,600m)
Hover ceiling IGE
9,845ft (3,000m)
Hover ceiling OGE
7,875ft (2,400m)
Range
200 miles (320km)

This is a three-seat helicopter designed as a general-purpose vehicle. It is equally suitable for police surveillance, as an ambulance, for pilot training, or for military observation, and also comes in an agricultural version (SH-4A), equipped with a boom and sprays.

The Siai-Marchetti company is a share-holder in Silvercraft and the principal provider of resources and factory space for production of the SH-4.

Japan Fuji/Fuji-Bell UH-1B

Engine
Lycoming KT5311A; 1,100shp
Rotor diameter
48ft 0in (16.63m)
Length overall
42ft 7¾in (13.00m)
Length of fuselage
38ft 4¾in (11.70m)
Weight empty
4,475lb (2,029kg)
Weight loaded
8,500lb (3,855kg)
Cruising speed
127mph (204km/h)
Rate of climb
2,060ft/m (628m)
Service ceiling
20,000ft (6,100m)
Hover ceiling IGE
14,500ft (4,420m)
Hover ceiling OGE
12,000ft (3,660m)
Range
252 miles (405km)

The military version of the 204B is this UH-1B; similar to the Bell variant (shown in picture), except for the Kawasaki-built engine. Fugi has modified the UH-1B to include wings and an extra stabiliser. This two-seat experimental helicopter (XMH) is equipped with fairings over the main rotor shaft and tail rotor gearbox. The skid-type landing gear is somewhat redesigned and the airframe has been reinforced. The new wings will span 22ft 3in (6.78m). Diameter of the main rotor for the XMH is 44ft (13.41m). Length overall is 42ft 7¾in (13.00m); weight loaded 7,606lb (3,450kg). The XMH's maximum speed currently is 157mph (252km/h).

Japan Fuji /Fuji-Bell 204B

Engine
Lycoming KT5311A ; 1,100shp
Rotor diameter
48ft 0in (16.63m)
Length overall
44ft 7¾in (13.61m)
Length of fuselage
40ft 4¾in (12.31m)
Weight empty
4,700lb (2,131kg)
Weight loaded
8,500lb (3,855kg)
Cruising speed
127mph (204km/h)
Rate of climb
1,730ft/m (527m)
Service ceiling
20,000ft (6,100m)
Hover ceiling IGE
18,000ft (5,485m)
Hover ceiling OGE
13,000ft (3,960m)
Range
252 miles (405km)

This is the civilian version of the Bell and Agusta 204B which is produced by Fuji for the Mitsui company. The craft is operated by Asahi Helicopter Company and All Nippon Airways. Its effectiveness in policing duties may be attested by its service with the Tokyo Police and the National Police Bureau. The Lycoming turboshaft power plant is Kawasaki-built.

Japan Kawasaki/KH-4

Engine
Lycoming TVO-435-D1A;
270hp
Rotor diameter
37ft 1½in (11.32m)
Length overall
43ft 2½in (13.17m)
Length of fuselage
32ft 7¼in (9.93m)
Weight empty
1,890lb (857kg)
Weight loaded
2,850lb (1,292kg)
Cruising speed
87mph (140km/h)
Rate of climb
850ft/m (260m)
Service ceiling
18,500ft (5,640m)
Hover ceiling IGE
18,000ft (5,485m)
Hover ceiling OGE
15,000ft (4,570m)
Range
214 miles (345km)

This company is a large
producer, under licence, of
American-developed aircraft,
particularly those of Bell,
Boeing Vertol, and Hughes.
    The KH-4 is a four-seat
helicopter developed from the
four-seater Bell 47G-3B.
Changes, in addition to the
space for an extra seat, include
new instrument and control
panels, and facility for increased

fuel capacity (46 imperial
gallons; 209 litres.
    The helicopter's duties can be
diversified with equipment such
as pontoons, ambulance
stretchers, and agricultural
spray gear.

Japan Kawasaki/Kawasaki-Vertol 107/II-2

Engine
Two (2) General Electric
CT58-110-1; 1,250shp
Rotor diameter
50ft 0in (15.24m)
Length overall
83ft 4in (25.40m)
Length of fuselage
44ft 7in (13.59m)
Weight empty
10,732lb (4,868kg)
Weight loaded
19,000lb (8,618kg)
Cruising speed
157mph (253km/h)
Rate of climb
1,440ft/m (439m)
Service ceiling
13,000ft (3,960m)
Hover ceiling IGE
8,400ft (2,560m)
Hover ceiling OGE
6,600ft (2,012m)
Range
109 miles (175km)

In the 1960s, Kawasaki obtained exclusive rights from Boeing to manufacture the 107 Model II transport helicopter, which it now offers in eight versions. The basic variation (the Boeing shown in picture) has been manufactured for civil operation in Thailand, Japan and the USA, where it is operated by Pan American Airways and New York Airways. Kawasaki also employs the 107/II-2 as test aircraft for the company.

In its other variations, the 107/II is employed in mine-sweeping operations by the Japan military services, and on search and rescue work by the Japanese and Swedish navies. For search and rescue (107/II-5), Sweden has replaced the Kawasaki engine with Rolls-Royce Bristol Gnome H.1200 turboshafts and a Decca navigation system.

54

Poland WSK-Swidnik /Mi-2

Engine
Two (2) Isotov GTD-350;
437shp
Rotor diameter
47ft 6¾in (14.50m)
Length overall
57ft 2in (17.42m)
Length of fuselage
37ft 4¾in (11.40m)
Weight empty
5,213lb (2,365kg)
Weight loaded
7,826lb (3,550kg)
Cruising speed
124mph (200km/h)
Rate of climb
885ft/m (270m)
Service ceiling
13,755ft (4,200m)
Hover ceiling IGE
6,550ft (2,000m)
Hover ceiling OGE
3,275ft (1,000m)
Range
360 miles (580km)

This twin-turbine light utility helicopter is of Soviet-design, licensed by the Poles who started its production in 1965.

The original Soviet version was designated SM-1 ten years earlier. Upon completion of all development and production, subsequent production and marketing rights were assigned to WSK-Swidnik, which has plans to continue its development through 1975.

The Mi-2's production versions are: cargo, passenger, ambulance, search and rescue and agricultural.

U.S.A. Bell /AH-1G HueyCobra

Engine
Lycoming T53-L-13; derated
to 1,100shp
Rotor diameter
44ft 0in (13.41m)
Length overall
52ft 11½in (16.14m)
Length of fuselage
44ft 5in (13.54m)
Weight empty
6,073lb (2,754kg)
Weight loaded
9,500lb (4,309kg)
Cruising speed
219mph (352km/h)
Rate of climb
1,230ft/m (375m)
Service ceiling
11,400ft (3,475m)
Hover ceiling IGE
9,900ft (3,015m)
Range
357 miles (574km)

A Model 209, this is the first attack helicopter in United States military combat history. Its primary mission is fire support of ground operations. The HueyCobra was developed as a fire-support aircraft for ground missions in Vietnam.

It is basically a small aircraft whose subdued silhouette and profile are designed for concealment and surprise attack in jungle areas. A gunship version (the AH-1Q) is equipped with TOW missiles, developed by the Hughes Aircraft Co.

Engine
Pratt & Whitney T400-CP-400;
1,250shp
Rotor diameter
44ft 0in (13.41m)
Length overall
53ft 4in (16.26m)
Length of fuselage
44ft 7in (13.59m)
Weight empty
9,637lb (4,371kg)
Weight loaded
10,000lb (4,535kg)
Cruising speed
207mph (333km/h)
Rate of climb
1,090ft/m (332m)
Service ceiling
10,550ft (3,215m)
Hover ceiling IGE
12,450ft (3,794m)
Range
359 miles (577km)

Also a Model 209, this is the United States Marine Corps' version of the Army's AH-1G, delivery of which began in 1970. In 1972, the U.S. Army funded an order for over two hundred aircraft for transfer by the United States government to Iran.

The AH-1J is equipped with a 20mm, electrically-operated turret; its increased gross weight supports armament loads of 2,200lb (1,000kg) externally and 542lb (247kg) internally. Its high-thrust tractor tail rotor permits hovering flight in crosswinds up to 40 knots.

U.S.A. Bell /HH-1K

Engine
Lycoming T53-L-13 ; derated
to 1,100shp
Rotor diameter
44ft 0in (13.41m)
Length overall
53ft 0in (16.15m)
Length of fuselage
38ft 5in (11.70m)
Weight empty
5,811lb (2,635kg)
Weight loaded
9,500lb (4,309kg)
Maximum speed
161mph (259km/h)
Rate of climb
1,160ft/m (353m)
Service ceiling
10,000ft (3,050m)
Hover ceiling IGE
10,400ft (3,170m)
Hover ceiling OGE
7,400ft (2,255m)
Range
312 miles (502km)

The United States Navy's
designation for a sea-air rescue
version of Bell's Model 204. Its
airframe resembles the Marine
Corps UH-1E. Orders for the
HH-1K were placed for deliveries
in the 1970s and equipment
includes a variety of sophisticated
electronic gear.

U.S.A. Bell /OH-13S

Engine
Lycoming TVO-435-25 ; 260hp
Rotor diameter
37ft 1⅛in (11.31m)
Length overall
43ft 2½in (13.17m)
Length of fuselage
32ft 6in (9.90m)
Weight empty
2,203lb (999kg)
Weight loaded
2,850lb (1,293kg)
Cruising speed
83mph (133km/h)
Rate of climb
550ft/m (168m)
Service ceiling
18,500ft (5,640m)
Hover ceiling IGE
18,000ft (5,500m)
Hover ceiling OGE
14,800ft (4,510m)
Range
250 miles (402km)

The United States Army's version of the Bell Model 47 (47G-3B), nicknamed the 'Sioux', is this observation helicopter powered by a 260hp Lycoming engine (TVO-435-25).

U.S.A. Bell/OH-58A Kiowa

Engine
Allison T63-A-700; 317shp
Rotor diameter
35ft 4in (10.77m)
Length overall
40ft 11¾in (12.49m)
Length of fuselage
32ft 7in (9.93m)
Weight empty
1,464lb (664kg)
Weight loaded
3,000lb (1,360kg)
Cruising speed
117mph (188km/h)
Rate of climb
1,780ft/m (543m)
Service ceiling
18,900ft (5,760m)
Hover ceiling IGE
13,600ft (4,145m)
Hover ceiling OGE
8,800ft (2,682m)
Range
305 miles (490km)

This turbine-powered aircraft was the winner of a light observation helicopter competition for the United States Army's mission in the Vietnam war. It was subsequently ordered by the Canadian military services and in 1972 a co-production arrangement was made with the Australian government.

The OH-58A Kiowa is similar to the Jet Ranger series, except for a larger main rotor diameter and diverse types of avionics. It is a five-place helicopter, and when not performing observation missions can be utilised in transport and utility functions.

For its battle function, it carries an XM-27E gun system and 2,000 rounds of ammunition.

U.S.A. Bell/TH-1L

Engine
Lycoming T53-L-13; 1,400shp
Rotor diameter
44ft 0in (13.41m)
Length overall
53ft 0in (16.15m)
Length of fuselage
38ft 5in (11.70m)
Weight empty
5,686lb (2,579kg)
Weight loaded
9,500lb (4,309kg)
Cruising speed
144mph (231km/h)
Rate of climb
1,160ft/m (353m)
Service ceiling
10,000ft (3,050m)
Hover ceiling IGE
10,400ft (3,170m)
Hover ceiling OGE
7,400ft (2,255m)
Range
312 miles (502km)

This is the United States Navy's training version of Bell's Model 204. The TH-1L is similar to the Marine Corps assault helicopter UH-1E (which has a personnel hoist and rotor brake), but with improved electronics and a 1,400shp Lycoming engine.

U.S.A. Bell /TH-13T

Engine
Lycoming TVO-435-D1B;
270hp
Rotor diameter
37ft 1⅛in (11.31m)
Length overall
43ft 2½in (13.17m)
Length of fuselage
32ft 6in (9.90m)
Weight empty
2,499lb (1,133kg)
Weight loaded
2,950lb (1,338kg)
Cruising speed
83mph (133km/h)
Rate of climb
990ft/m (302m)
Service ceiling
16,800ft (5,120m)
Hover ceiling IGE
16,000ft (4,875m)
Hover ceiling OGE
10,500ft (3,200m)
Range
250 miles (402km)

The TH-13T is the twin-seat
instrument-trainer variant of
Bell's Model 47 (47G-3B-1)
equipped with additional
electronic devices, including
beacon receiver, compass and
gyro system, and a blind-flying
hood.

Engine
Allison 250-C81 ; 270shp
Rotor diameter
33ft 4in (10.16m)
Length overall
38ft 9½in (11.82m)
Weight empty
2,114lb (062kg)
Weight loaded
2,900lb (1,318kg)
Rate of climb
1,030ft/m (310m)
Maximum airspeed
130mph (210km/h)
Service ceiling
16,000ft (4,880m)
Hover ceiling IGE
8,700ft (2,650m)
Hover ceiling OGE
4,200ft (1,280m)
Range
330 miles (210km)

A turbine-powered helicopter, the TH-57A SeaRanger is used to train every United States Navy recruit who embarks on primary helicopter training. The basic equipment includes standard Navy avionics in addition to fluids, mission equipment, and accommodation for a crew of three.

Engine
Lycoming T53-L-11 ; 1,100shp
Rotor diameter
44ft 0in (13.41m)
Length overall
53ft 0in (16.15m)
Length of fuselage
38ft 5in (11.70m)
Weight empty
5,071lb (2,300kg)
Weight loaded
9,500lb (4,309kg)
Cruising speed
148mph (238km/h)
Rate of climb
1,400ft/m (425m)
Service ceiling
11,500ft (3,500m)
Hover ceiling IGE
10,600ft (3,230m)
Hover ceiling OGE
10,000ft (3,050m)
Range
382 miles (615km)

The Model 204, in the mid 1950s, was Bell's winning entry in the United States Army's design competition for a utility helicopter whose services would include casualty-evacuation and instrument-training. The production version, UH-1A, was nicknamed the 'Huey' and subsequently saw service in Vietnam, where it was fitted with air-to-surface rockets and machine-guns.

In 1965, Bell's turbo-engined UH-1C revealed a 'door-hinge' rotor (Model 540), whose increased chord resulted in corresponding increases in speed and manoeuvrability. Reduction in vibrations and stress, facilitated by the 540, have served to release previous inhibitions on maximum speed potential.

U.S.A. Bell /UH-1D

Engine
Lycoming T53-L-11 ; 1,100shp
Rotor diameter
48ft (14.63m)
Length overall
57ft 1in (17.40m)
Length of fuselage
41ft 10¾in (12.77m)
Weight empty
4,939lb (2,240kg)
Weight loaded
9,500lb (4,309kg)
Cruising speed
127mph (204km/h)
Rate of climb
1,600ft/m (488m)
Service ceiling
12,600ft (3,840m)
Hover ceiling IGE
13,600ft (4,145m)
Hover ceiling OGE
1,100ft (335m)
Range
318 miles (511km)

This is one of the Bell Model 205 family, and resembles the earlier Model 204 except for a longer fuselage and increased passenger capacity. In the UH-1D, which is the U.S. Army's version of the Iroquois, the fuel spaces have been re-located in order to make room for a pilot and twelve troops. In the ambulance version, six stretchers and an attendant can be accommodated.

The West German company, Dornier, has built 352 of these helicopters for the German Army and Air Force under licence from Bell.

U.S.A. Bell /UH-1E

Engine
Lycoming T53-L-11 ; 1,100shp
Rotor diameter
44ft 0in (13.41m)
Length overall
53ft 0in (16.15m)
Length of fuselage
38ft 5in (11.70m)
Weight empty
5,055lb (2,293kg)
Weight loaded
9,500lb (4,309kg)
Cruising speed
138mph (222km/h)
Rate of climb
1,849ft/m (563m)
Service ceiling
21,000ft (6,400m)
Hover ceiling IGE
15,800ft (4,815m)
Hover ceiling OGE
11,800ft (3,595m)
Range
286 miles (460km)

This model of the Bell 204
family was chosen in the early
1960s by the U.S. Marine Corps
to replace the Kaman OH-43D.
The Model 540 rotor, introduced
on the Army's UH-1C, was
fitted to this Marine Corps
version in 1965, in addition to
7.65mm M-60 machine-guns
and rockets for the UH-1E's
mission as a troop-carrier and
escort in the Vietnam war.

U.S.A. Bell/UH-1F

Engine
General Electric T58-GE-3;
1,272shp
Rotor diameter
44ft 0in (13.41m)
Length overall
53ft 0in (16.15m)
Length of fuselage
38ft 5in (11.70m)
Weight empty
5,071lb (2,300kg)
Weight loaded
9,500lb (4,309kg)
Cruising speed
148mph (238km/h)
Rate of climb
1,230ft/m (375m)
Service ceiling
13,450ft (4,100m)
Hover ceiling IGE
10,300ft (3,139m)
Hover ceiling OGE
4,000ft (1,219m)
Range
347 miles (558km)

The UH-1F was the U.S. Air
Force's choice of the Bell
Model 204, but powered by a
1,272shp General Electric
turboshaft engine (T58-GE-3).
  The helicopter is used in
missile site support activities,
where it can manage up to
4,000lb (1,815kg) of cargo. In
normal flight, it will
accommodate a pilot and up to
fourteen passengers. The

UH-1F can also be equipped
with an antenna to detect
low-flying aircraft, the antenna
being retracted and rotated by
means of two electric motors.
  Several UH-1F helicopters
were modified for use in classified psychological warfare in
Vietnam. A variant, TH-1F, is
used for training personnel in
the handling of instruments
and hoists.

U.S.A. Bell /UH-1H Iroquois

Engine
Lycoming T53-L-13 ; 1,400shp
Rotor diameter
48ft 0in (14.63m)
Length overall
57ft 1in (17.40m)
Length of fuselage
41ft 10¾in (12.77m)
Weight empty
4,667lb (2,116kg)
Weight loaded
9,500lb (4,309kg)
Cruising speed
127mph (204km/h)
Rate of climb
1,600ft/m (488m)
Service ceiling
12,600ft (3,840m)
Hover ceiling IGE
13,600ft (4,145m)
Hover ceiling OGE
1,100ft (335m)
Range
318 miles (511km)

The Model 204 was the winner, in 1956, of a U.S. Army design competition, and was given the name 'Iroquois' for American and Canadian military service. Out of the earlier model evolved the 205 with a larger fuselage and increased cabin space.

The UH-1H has a two-blade semi-rigid main rotor ; its fuselage is all-metal, semi-monococque. The turboshaft engine is mounted in back of the transmission and enclosed in cowlings.

China has concluded a licensing agreement to produce the UH-1H for its armed forces.

U.S.A. Bell /UH-1N

Engine
Pratt & Whitney PTCT-3
Turbo-Twin Pac; 1,100shp
Rotor diameter
48ft 2¼in (14.69m)
Length overall
57ft 3¼in (17.46m)
Length of fuselage
42ft 4¾in (12.29m)
Weight loaded
10,500lb (4,762kg)
Cruising speed
126mph (203km/h)
Rate of climb
1,745ft/m (532m)
Service ceiling
15,000ft (4,570m)
Hover ceiling IGE
12,900ft (3,930m)
Hover ceiling OGE
4,900ft (1,495m)
Range
248 miles (400km)

The military version of the 212 has the same configuration as the Bell 205A and UH-1H airframe, but differs in the avionics package it presents. The helicopter was designed for use by the Navy, Marine Corps and Canadian armed services, and its external cargo load capability is 3,383lb (1,534kg).

In 1972, a UH-1N in the Antarctic carried a parachute rigger to a height of 20,500ft (6,248m). The subsequent parachute jump set a new record for that frozen continent.

U.S.A. Bell /47G-3B-2A

Engine
Lycoming TVO-435-F1A ; 280hp
Rotor diameter
37ft 1½in (11.32m)
Length overall
43ft 7½in (13.30m)
Length of fuselage
31ft 7in (9.63m)
Weight empty
1,893lb (858kg)
Weight loaded
2,950lb (1,338kg)
Cruising speed
84mph (135km/h)
Rate of climb
990ft/m (302m)
Service ceiling
19,000ft (5,790m)
Hover ceiling IGE
17,700ft (5,395m)
Hover ceiling OGE
12,700ft (3,870m)
Range
247 miles (397km)

The Model 47, first produced in 1946, resulted in the award by America's Civil Aeronautics Administration of the world's first commercial helicopter licence. The series is now one of the most productive of the entire Bell line.

This is a three-seat utility helicopter, a commercial version of the original Model 47, with a record of high-altitude performances in a wide range of temperatures. Manoeuvrability is facilitated by a 10lb (4.5kg) weight fitted to each blade.

U.S.A. Bell /47G-4A

Engine
Lycoming VO-540-B1B3;
280hp
Rotor diameter
37ft 1⅛in (11.31m)
Length overall
43ft 2½in (13.17m)
Length of fuselage
32ft 6in (9.90m)
Weight empty
1,880lb (852kg)
Weight loaded
2,950lb (1,338kg)
Cruising speed
89mph (143km/h)
Rate of climb
800ft/m (244m)
Service ceiling
11,200ft (3,415m)
Hover ceiling IGE
7,700ft (2,347m)
Range
259 miles (417km)

Another commercial version of
the Bell Model 47 family; a
three-seat utility helicopter. Its
flight controls are hydraulically
spurred, and the airframe is
approved for 1,200-hour
intervals between overhauls.
In 1969, Pacific Southwest
Airlines set an unofficial
helicopter endurance record of
121 hours with one of these
aircraft.

U.S.A. Bell /47G-5A

Engine
Lycoming VO-435-B1A ; 265hp
Rotor diameter
37ft 1½in (11.32m)
Length overall
43ft 7½in (13.30m)
Length of fuselage
31ft 7in (9.63m)
Weight empty
1,732lb (785kg)
Weight loaded
2,850lb (1,293kg)
Cruising speed
85mph (137km/h)
Rate of climb
860ft/m (262m)
Service ceiling
10,500ft (3,200m)
Hover ceiling IGE
5,900ft (1,800m)
Hover ceiling OGE
1,400ft (427m)
Range
256 miles (411km)

Like the 47G-3B-2A, this is a three-seat utility helicopter with a larger cabin than its predecessor G-5. Standard items of equipment include a tinted Plexiglas canopy, a synchronised elevator and two 28.5 U.S. gallon (108 litre) fuel tanks.

As in most 47G models, the Bell 'AgMaster' chemical system can be quickly fitted by two people for a swift spray service in agricultural areas.

U.S.A. Bell /205A-1

Engine
Lycoming T53-L-13 ; 1,400shp
Rotor diameter
48ft 0in (14.63m)
Length overall
57ft 1in (17.40m)
Length of fuselage
41ft 6in (12.65m)
Weight empty
5,197lb (2,357kg)
Weight loaded
10,500lb (4,763kg)
Cruising speed
127mph (204km/h)
Rate of climb
1,680ft/m (512m)
Service ceiling
14,700ft (4,480m)
Hover ceiling IGE
10,400ft (3,170m)
Hover ceiling OGE
6,000ft (1,830m)
Range
344 miles (553km)

A development from the UH-1H Iroquois, this helicopter has been designed for rapid conversion for freight, ambulance, rescue or executive transport functions.

The 205A-1 has space for fifteen passengers and can be adapted to accommodate six stretchers and two medical attendants. It differs from the UH-1H in the wide range of its optional items which include a 360-channel VHF transceiver and intercom system, external cargo suspensions, a rescue hoist and customised interiors.

Agusta, of Italy, has been licensed to produce the 205A-1.

Engine
Allison 250-C20 ; 400shp
Rotor diameter
33ft 4in (10.16m)
Length overall
38ft 9½in (11.82m)
Length of fuselage
31ft 2in (9.50m)
Weight empty
1,455lb (660kg)
Weight loaded
3,200lb (1,451kg)
Cruising speed
138mph (222km/h)
Rate of climb
1,260ft/m (384m)
Service ceiling
20,000ft (6,095m)
Hover ceiling IGE
11,300ft (3,445m)
Hover ceiling OGE
5,800ft (1,770m)
Range
388 miles (624km)

A light observation helicopter which became a replacement for the 206A following installation of a turbine engine designed for more powerful performances under high-altitude conditions.

Bell has also announced a demonstration model in which the fuselage would be suspended from a nodalised beam.

The landing gear has a tubular steel skid to protect the rotor in a tail-first descent. The two main rotor blades of aluminium-alloy do not normally fold but can be modified to do so if required. A rotor brake is available as an optional item.

Engine
Allison 250-C20B ; 420shp
Rotor diameter
37ft 0in (11.02m)
Length overall
42ft 5in (12.93m)
Length of fuselage
31ft 2in (9.50m)
Weight loaded
3,900lb (178kg)
Cruising speed
136mph (216km/h)
Service ceiling
12,700ft (3,874m)
Hover ceiling IGE
8,200ft (2,500m)
Hover ceiling OGE
2,000ft (610m)
Range
430 miles (688km)

This seven-seater, turbine-engined helicopter is under development with first deliveries planned for 1975-6. It will be the first production model to incorporate Bell's Noda-Matic transmission suspension system which isolates structure-borne noise from cabin environs through the use of elastometrics.

The LongRanger's 83cuft of cabin space is designed to accommodate passengers with skis, surveying transits, tent-poles, and other odd-shaped items of equipment not ordinarily transportable in more

conventional light craft.

Available kits will include emergency flotation gear and a cargo hook with a capacity of 2,000lb. Bell engineers are working on an optional environmental control unit, powered by bleed air, which will provide heat in winter and air-conditioning in summer.

U.S.A. Bell /212

Engine
Pratt & Whitney PT6T-3
Turbo-Twin Pac; 1,100shp
Rotor diameter
48ft 2¼in (14.69m)
Length overall
57ft 3¼in (17.46m)
Length of fuselage
42ft 4¾in (12.92m)
Weight empty
5,549lb (2,517kg)
Weight loaded
11,200lb (5,080kg)
Cruising speed
126mph (203km/h)
Rate of climb
1,745ft/m (532m)
Service ceiling
17,400ft (5,305m)
Hover ceiling IGE
14,700ft (4,480m)
Hover ceiling OGE
10,600ft (3,230m)
Range
273 miles (439km)

A twin-engined helicopter developed from the UH-1 for civil and military usage. Both versions can accommodate a pilot and up to fourteen passengers. The 212's conversion to IFR configuration resulted in a new and diversified avionics package. Subsequently, several aircraft were purchased by a Norwegian concern to support its offshore oil operations in

the North Sea.
   The 212 can provide 220cuft (6.23m³) cargo space and carry an external load of 5,000lb (2,268kg).

U.S.A. Bell /214A

Engine
Lycoming LTC4B-8D ; 2,930shp
Rotor diameter
50ft 0in (15.25m)
Length overall
45ft 8¾in (13.75m)
Weight empty
7,550lb (3,432kg)
Weight loaded
15,000lb (6,814kg)
**Maximum design
true air speed**
172mph (275km/h)

A new advanced utility helicopter, 287 of which were ordered by Iran through the United States Government, for delivery starting in 1975. On the same contract, Iran also purchased 202 AH-1J SeaCobras, the value of the total procurement exceeding five hundred million dollars.

The 214A will also be modified for commercial operation (and designated Model 214B) by the addition of an engine fire-extinguishing system, push-out (escape) windows in the cargo doors, commercial avionics, and a crashworthy fuel system—a first in a commercial helicopter.

The 214 fuselage is designed to withstand 3½ Gs at 10,500lb gross weight. Missions for the 214A will include troop

transport, internal and external cargo transport, and air ambulance duties. The helicopter will carry fourteen troops and a two-man crew, plus 1,372lb of fuel. In ambulance configuration, it will accommodate six stretchers and crew.

Engine
Pratt & Whitney T400-CP-400;
1,800shp
Rotor diameter
48ft 0in (14.63m)
Length of fuselage
49ft 0in (14.93m)
Weight loaded
14,000lb (6,350kg)
Maximum speed
230mph (370km/h)
Hover ceiling OGE
4,000ft (1,220m)

Bell has completed a prototype of this advanced armed helicopter, which is patterned on the Navy's AH-1J SeaCobra. Although of similar configuration the KingCobra has a longer fuselage and an improved main rotor. It has been modified to include a stabilised multi-sensor sight and larger ammunition bay. The maximum diving speed, in its first test, exceeded 230mph (370km/h).

U.S.A. Boeing Vertol /CH /UH-46A

Engines
Two (2) General Electric
T58-GE-8B ; 1,250shp
Rotor diameter
50ft 0in (15.24m)
Length overall
83ft 4in (25.40m)
Length of fuselage
44ft 10in (13.66m)
Weight empty
12,406lb (5,627kg)
Weight loaded
21,400lb (9,706kg)
Cruising speed
155mph (249km/h)
Rate of climb
1,439ft/m (438.7m)
Service ceiling
13,000ft (3,960m)
Hover ceiling IGE
9,070ft (2,765m)
Hover ceiling OGE
5,600ft (1,707m)
Range
230 miles (370km)

The CH-46A was originally designed in the mid-1950s by Vertol Aircraft Corporation as the forerunner of the Model 107 series. In 1960 Vertol became a division of The Boeing Company and, following a U.S. Marine Corps competition in 1961 for a medium assault/transport helicopter, the Boeing Vertol 107M was given the military designation of 'Sea Knight'. In 1962 the designation became CH-46A after its first flight demonstration. By the summer of 1965 delivery of the craft had been made to five Marine Corps squadrons.

The helicopter has an all-metal fuselage of semi-monocoque construction. Its two rotors are triple-bladed and interchangeable. A shaft extends through the entire cabin and up to the front rotor. There is a side entry and a rear-loading ramp.

In 1964 the U.S. Navy adopted the CH-46A for replenishment of combat vessels at sea. Production has continued into the 1970s and a mine-hunting and mine-sweeping version has been designated RH-46A.

Accommodation is provided for a crew of three and up to 25 troops, or 15 stretchers and two medical attendants.

Engines
Two (2) General Electric
T58-GE-10; 1,400shp
Rotor diameter
51ft 0in (15.54m)
Length overall
84ft 4in (25.70m)
Length of fuselage
44ft 10in (13.66m)
Weight empty
13,067lb (5,927kg)
Weight loaded
23,000lb (10,433kg)
Cruising speed
165mph (266km/h)
Rate of climb
1,715ft/m (523m)
Service ceiling
14,000ft (4,265m)
Hover ceiling IGE
9,500ft (2,895m)
Range
228 miles (367km)

The 46D and 46F are developed
versions of the CH-46A, with
engine power increased from
1,250shp to 1,400shp. These
helicopters have been used by
the U.S. Navy and Marine
Corps as assault and logistics
support craft in Vietnam, in
addition to seeing service in
Atlantic, Pacific and
Mediterranean waters.

U.S.A. Boeing Vertol/CH-47A Chinook

Development undertaken in 1956 by Department of the Army for turbine-powered helicopters to replace piston-engined transports. Production coincided with the start of the war in Vietnam, where the CH-47A was used for movement of troops, artillery, ammunition, fuel and other cargo. In 1971, operations of the CH-47A were undertaken by the Vietnamese Air Force.

Engine
Lycoming T55-L-5; 2,200shp
Rotor diameter
59ft 1¼in (18.02m)
Length overall
98ft 0⅓in (29.90m)
Length of fuselage
51ft 0in (15.54m)
Weight empty
17,932lb (8,133kg)
Weight loaded
28,400lb (12,882kg)
Cruising speed
150mph (241km/h)
Rate of climb
2,180ft/m (644m)
Service ceiling
11,900ft (3,625m)
Hover ceiling OGE
12,500ft (3,810m)

U.S.A. Boeing Vertol/CH-47B Chinook

Engine
Lycoming T55-L-7C ; 2,850shp
Rotor diameter
60ft 0in (18.29m)
Length overall
99ft 0in (30.18m)
Length of fuselage
51ft 0in (15.54m)
Weight empty
19,375lb (8,788kg)
Weight loaded
31,350lb (14,220kg)
Cruising speed
162mph (261km/h)
Rate of climb
2,225ft/m (678m)
Service ceiling
15,000ft (4,570m)
Hover ceiling OGE
12,400ft (3,780m)

Improvement to the speed and payload capabilities of the CH-47A resulted in the production of the 'B' model, which was first delivered to the U.S. Army in May 1967.

Two pilots are accommodated on the flight deck, with a jump seat for the crew chief, and seating spaces are available for up to 44 troops.

Total fuel capacity is 621 U.S. gallons (2,350 litres) ; total oil capacity 3.7 U.S. gallons (14 litres).

U.S.A. Boeing Vertol/CH-47C Chinook

Engine
Lycoming T55-L-11A;
3,750shp
Rotor diameter
60ft 0in (18.29m)
Length overall
99ft 0in (30.18m)
Length of fuselage
51ft 0in (15.54m)
Weight empty
20,378lb (9,243kg)
Weight loaded
39,200lb (17,781kg)
Cruising speed
160mph (257km/h)
Rate of climb
2,045ft/m (623m)
Service ceiling
10,200ft (3,110m)
Hover ceiling OGE
9,600ft (2,925m)

This latest model in the Chinook range was delivered to the U.S. Army in March 1969, and has since found markets among eight nations. In March 1972 the Royal Australian Air Force placed an order for twelve aircraft. In addition to its employment at U.S. Army and National Guard installations, it is now used extensively during floods, earthquakes etc.

The CH-47C, which is capable of lifting 12 tons, has a total fuel capacity of 1,129 U.S. gallons (4,273 litres).

Engine
Two (2) General Electric
T58-GE-8B; 1,250shp
Rotor diameter
50ft 0in (15.54m)
Length overall
83ft 4in (25.40m)
Length of fuselage
44ft 7in (13.59m)
Weight empty
11,251lb (5,104kg)
Weight loaded
21,400lb (9,706kg)
Cruising speed
157mph (253km/h)
Rate of climb
1,525ft/m (465m)
Service ceiling
14,000ft (4,265m)
Hover ceiling IGE
9,800ft (2,985m)
Range
665 miles (1,070km)

The CH-113 is a military version
of the Model 107 built in the
United States for export.
Sweden has purchased the
helicopter for its Army's search
and rescue missions, while in
Canada the CH-113 'Labrador'
is used for Air Force transport
duty, and the CH-113A
'Voyager' for the Navy's cargo
movements. Boeing Vertol has
granted a licence to Kawasaki,
of Japan, for the production of
military versions.

Engine
Three (3) Allison T701-AD-700;
8,000hp
Rotor diameter
92ft 0in (28.04m)
Length overall
162ft 3in (49.45m)
Length of fuselage
89ft 3in (27.20m)
Wheel track
25ft 0in (7.62m)
Wheelbase
40ft 11½in (12.48m)
Weight empty
59,580lb (27,025kg)
Design gross weight
118,000lb (53,640kg)
Alternate gross weight
148,000lb (67,130kg)

The XCH-62 was Boeing-Vertol's successful proposal in a 1971 U.S. Department of Defence 76 million dollar competition for first-phase development of a heavy-lift helicopter. Primary mission is a 22½ ton payload for two 25 nautical miles radii round-trip missions. Alternate gross weight of 148,000lb (67,130kg) will allow the helicopter to carry up to 35 tons payload. One potential application is the offshore discharge of container ships.

On 5 September 1974, an aviation 'first' was achieved by

the successful demonstration of a pure 'fly-by-wire' flight control system, wherein the pilot's only means of control was by electric signals transmitted between the cockpit and the hydraulic actuators which control the forward and aft rotor blades. The 'fly-by-wire' system uses electric signals to replace the mechanical push-pull rods, bell cranks/cables and pulleys used on conventional aircraft.

Engine
Two (2) General Electric
T700-GE-700; 1,500shp

In 1972 Boeing Vertol and
Sikorsky Aircraft were selected
by the U.S. Army to design,
build and test three prototype
aircraft for its Utility Tactical
Transport Aircraft System
(UTTAS).

The UTTAS helicopter is a
turboshaft twin-engine, single-
rotor craft designed to carry a
crew of three and eleven troops.
Its planned functions are troop
transport, medical evacuation
and logistics. The helicopter is
scheduled to replace the
UH-1H Huey in the assault
transport role in the late 1970s.

After competitive flight trials
between the Boeing and
Sikorsky prototypes, a production
contract is anticipated in the
mid-1970s.

The Model 179 is Boeing Vertol's commercial designation of its UTTAS (U.S. Army's Utility Tactical Transport Aircraft System) design. This civil helicopter is a twin-turbine, single-rotor craft in the 15,000lb gross weight class with full IFR (Instrument Flight Regulations) capability—aimed at achieving high reliability and safety, low vibration and noise levels, and lower operating costs.

U.S.A. Boeing Vertol /107-II

Engine
Two (2) General Electric CT 58;
1,250shp
Rotor diameter
50ft 0in (15.24m)
Length overall
83ft 4in (25.40m)
Length of fuselage
44ft 7in (13.59m)
Weight empty
10,732lb (4,868kg)
Weight loaded
19,000lb (8,618kg)
Cruising speed
157mph (253km/h)
Rate of climb
1,440ft/m (439m)
Service ceiling
350ft (107m)
Hover ceiling IGE
8,400ft (2,560m)
Hover ceiling OGE
6,600ft (2,012m)
Range
109 miles (175km)

This is the commercial version of the Boeing Vertol 'Sea Knight', built in the early 1960s to meet the requirements of New York Airways, which operates passenger helicopter services in the Metropolitan New York area. The Model 107 has a sealed landing gear and fuel-cell stubs to reinforce stability. Its stability augmentation system (SAS) ensures operation under all weather conditions.

Engine
Lycoming IVO-360-A1A ; 180hp
Rotor diameter
23ft 9in (7.25m)
Length overall
23ft 9in (7.25m)
Length of fuselage
21ft 9¼in (6.90m)
Weight empty
1,020lb (463kg)
Weight loaded
1,670lb (758kg)
Cruising speed
100mph (161km/h)
Rate of climb
1,300ft/m (396m)
Service ceiling
11,400ft (3,475m)
Range
200 miles (322km)

A two-seat light utility helicopter, the B-2B was first developed in the 1950s as a conventional craft with extruded aluminum three-bladed main and tail rotors. Production models in the 1960s revealed redesigned and enlarged cockpits, and a fuel-injection engine. Inflated pontoons on a skid landing gear can be fitted for amphibious operation.

U.S.A. Enstrom/F-28A

Engine
Lycoming HIO-360-C1A;
205hp
Rotor diameter
32ft 0in (9.75m)
Length overall
29ft 4in (8.90m)
Weight empty
1,450lb (657kg)
Weight loaded
2,150lb (975kg)
Cruising speed
100mph (161km/h)
Rate of climb
950ft/m (290m)
Service ceiling
12,000ft (3,660m)
Hover ceiling IGE
6,000ft (1,825m)
Hover ceiling OGE
3,400ft (1,038m)
Range
237 miles (381km)

A three-seat light helicopter fitted with a fuel-injection Lycoming engine cooled by an axial flow fan. An auxiliary fuel pump is standard equipment, and a single wide belt with multiple grooves transmits power from the engine to the main rotor gearbox. An idler puller, affixed to the horizontally mounted engine, permits operation of the powerplant without turning the rotor.

The Enstrom Helicopter Corporation is also developing an advanced version of the F-28A, to be named 'Model 280 Shark'.

Engine
Allison 250-C18 ; 233shp
Rotor diameter
35ft 4¾in (10.79m)
Length overall
39ft 9½in (12.13m)
Length of fuselage
29ft 9½in (9.08m)
Weight empty
1,396lb (633kg)
Weight loaded
2,750lb (1,247kg)
Cruising speed
127mph (204km/h)
Rate of climb
1,600ft/m (488m)
Service ceiling
14,200ft (4,325m)
Hover ceiling IGE
13,400ft (4,085m)
Hover ceiling OGE
8,400ft (2,560m)
Range
348 miles (560km)

A development from the OH-5A, which had been the Fairchild-Hiller entry in the U.S. Army's competition for a light helicopter production programme (won in the mid-1960s by the Hughes Tool Co's OH-6A).

This turbine-powered helicopter seats a pilot and passenger up front, with seats in the rear for three more passengers. The two-bladed semi-rigid main rotor is all-metal, the double-bladed tail rotor is aluminum. The main rotor blades are not foldable.

The FH-1100 is multi-purpose, convertible for executive, ambulance and military usage. A wide range of armaments can be installed, including anti-submarine weapons.

U.S.A. Hughes /300

Engine
Lycoming HIO-360-A1A;
180hp
Rotor diameter
25ft 3½in (7.71m)
Length overall
28ft 10¾in (8.80m)
Length of fuselage
21ft 11¾in (6.80m)
Weight empty
958lb (434kg)
Weight loaded
1,670lb (757kg)
Cruising speed
80mph (129km/h)
Rate of climb
1,140ft/m (347m)
Service ceiling
13,000ft (3,960m)
Hover ceiling IGE
7,700ft (2,350m)
Hover ceiling OGE
5,800ft (1,770m)
Range
300 miles (480km)

In the mid-1950s, Hughes Helicopters developed a two-seat light helicopter designated Model 269. Subsequent versions included the TH-55A (a trainer for the U.S. Army's use in the Vietnam war) and the even more versatile 300 and 300C for a variety of civil purposes.

The three-seat 300 is distinctive for its quiet tail rotor, which has reduced the

helicopter's sound level by up to 80 per cent.

The basic configuration is still used by the U.S. Army as a trainer, but the 300 is equally viable for police patrol, fire control, agricultural spray and seeding, and land development surveys.

U.S.A. Hughes /300C

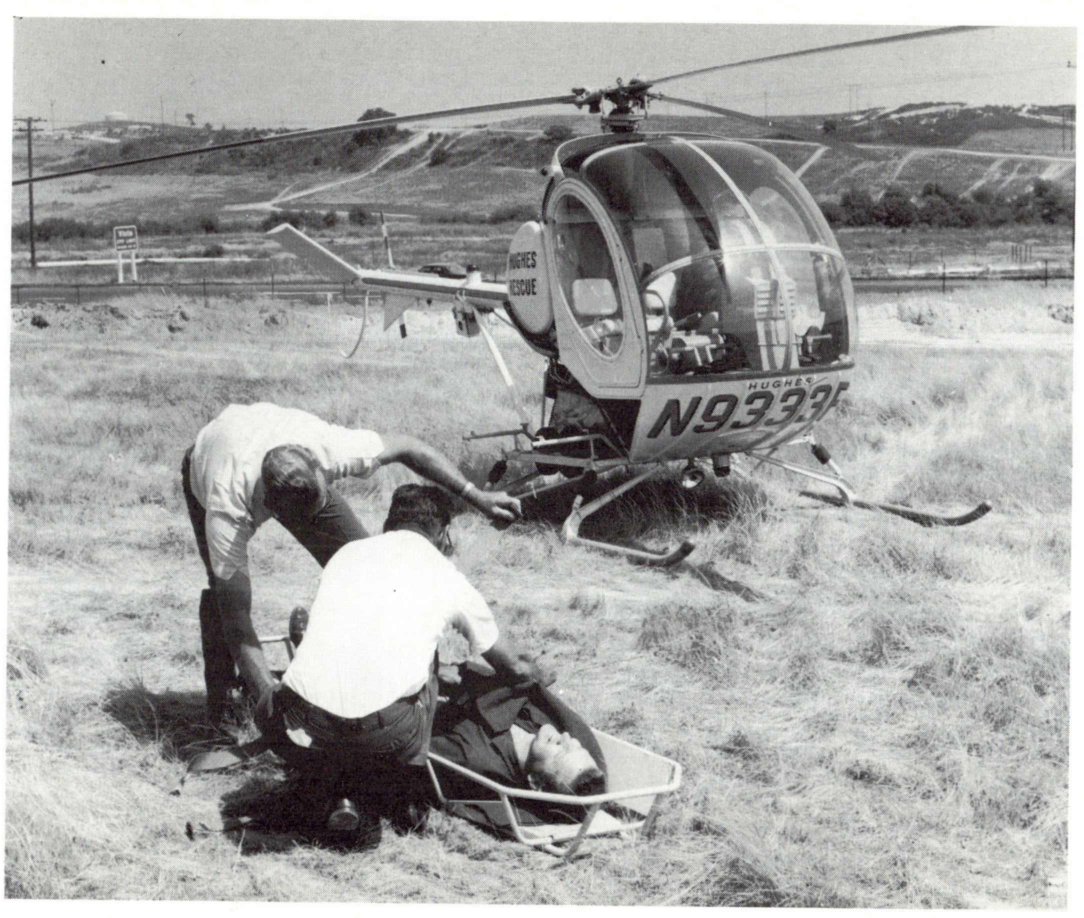

Engine
Lycoming HIO-360-D1A;
190hp
Rotor diameter
26ft 10in (8.18m)
Length overall
30ft 10in (9.42m)
Weight empty
1,039lb (471kg)
Weight loaded
1,900lb (861kg)
Cruising speed
100mph (161km/h)
Service ceiling
12,00ft (3,658m)
Hover ceiling IGE
6,900ft (2,103m)
Hover ceiling OGE
4,250ft (1,295m)
Range
232 miles (373km)

An improved version of the versatile 300, notably in the increased engine power and larger rotor diameter, resulting in a 41 per cent increase in the payload. An enlarged vertical stabiliser makes for improved handling and greater directional stability, while the longer and stronger tail boom allows for greater loads at reduced levels of vibration.

The 300C accommodates a pilot and two passengers seated side-by-side.

U.S.A. Hughes /500

Engine
Allison 250-C18A ; 243shp
Rotor diameter
26ft 4in (8.03m)
Length overall
30ft 3¾in (9.24m)
Length of fuselage
23ft 0in (7.01m)
Weight empty
1,088lb (493kg)
Weight loaded
3,000lb (1,360kg)
Cruising speed
135mph (217km/h)
Rate of climb
1,700ft/m (518m)
Service ceiling
14,400ft (4,390m)
Hover ceiling IGE
8,200ft (2,500m)
Hover ceiling OGE
5,300ft (1,615m)
Range
377 miles (606km)

The Model 500, the commercial version of the OH-6A, made its production debut in 1969. It has three basic mission designs : as a five-place executive transport ; a utility aircraft with seating for seven and capability for a 1,400lb load carried externally ; and as an international military helicopter.

The rear department of the 500C can accommodate two 55-gallon drums without the

use of special skids. Optional equipment comprises inflatable floats, personnel hoist, ambulance kit, and external baggage pods.

The 500M is the foreign military version, and has been sold to Argentina, Denmark, Japan, Mexico and Spain, among others.

U.S.A. Hughes /500C

Engine
Allison 250-C20 ; 400shp
Rotor diameter
26ft 3in (8.06m)
Length overall
30ft 3in (9.23m)
Length of fuselage
23ft 0in (7.01m)
Weight empty
1,240lb (563kg)
Weight loaded
2,550lb (1,160kg)
Cruising speed
145mph (232km/h)
Rate of climb
1,700ft/m (518m)
Service ceiling
14,500ft (4,422m)
Hover ceiling IGE
12,900ft (3,965m)
Hover ceiling OGE
6,700ft (2,050m)

The Hughes 500 light turbine helicopter can be converted from a de luxe 5-place executive transport to a utility cargo carrier, or a short-haul craft with seats for a pilot and six passengers. Typical usage is agricultural duty for seeding and spraying ; aerial survey, patrol and photography ; fire-fighting ; air-rescue ; tasks within the construction, petroleum and forestry industries.

The 1,300lb capacity rear

compartment has space for two 55-gallon drums without need for special skids or false floors. Outsize bulky loads can be carried externally by the cargo hook, which is rated for 1,800lb. Standard equipment includes barometric altimeter, magnetic compass, engine oil pressure indicator, and two anticollision Strobe lights. Optional equipment listed are VHF transceivers, inflatable floats, a stretcher kit, turn and bank indicator and dual controls.

U.S.A. Hughes/OH-6A

Engine
Allison T63-A-5A; 317shp
Rotor diameter
26ft 4in (8.03m)
Length overall
30ft 3¾in (9.24m)
Length of fuselage
23ft 0in (7.01m)
Weight empty
1,229lb (557kg)
Weight loaded
2,700lb (1,225kg)
Cruising speed
150mph (241km/h)
Rate of climb
1,840ft/m (560m)
Service ceiling
15,800ft (4,815m)
Hover ceiling IGE
11,800ft (3,595m)
Hover ceiling OGE
7,300ft (2,225m)
Range
380 miles (611km)

This was the winner of the U.S. Army's design competition in the 1960s for a light observation helicopter. Since then the OH-6A Cayuse has set twenty-three world records in diverse tests, including one for non-stop, California to Florida, 2,213 miles (3,562km) in a straight line.

Modifications on the turbine-powered OH-6A sponsored by the Advanced Research Project Agency (ARPA) of the U.S. Department of Defense has resulted in a helicopter which the company heralds as the quietest yet built.

The modifications included a change to a five-bladed main rotor, a four-bladed tail rotor, and exhaust muffler. The OH-6A's crew of two are seated side-by-side in front. Two additional seats in the cargo area can be folded to provide space for four soldiers.

U.S.A. Kamen /HH-43B Huskie

Engine
Lycoming T53-L-1B; 860shp
Rotor diameter
47ft 0in (14.33m)
Length of fuselage
25ft 2in (7.67m)
Weight empty
4,469lb (2,027kg)
Weight loaded
8,800lb (3,992kg)
Cruising speed
109mph (175km/h)
Service ceiling
25,000ft (7.622m)
Hover ceiling IGE
19,000ft (5,486m)
Hover ceiling OGE
15,000ft (4,572m)
Range
270 miles (435km)

Charles H. Kamen, now President and Chairman of the of the Aerospace Kamen Corporation, developed in 1945 a servo-flap control system for helicopter rotors. The HH-43 Huskie, which resulted from the initial research, subsequently became the U.S. Air Force's first turbine-powered helicopter; the setter of eight world records and a significant vehicle in search-and-rescue activities. Since 1960, HH-43s have been credited with the rescue of more than 5,155 persons.

U.S.A. Kamen /HH-43F Huskie

Engine
Lycoming T53-L-11A; 1,100shp
Rotor diameter
47ft 0in (14.33m)
Length of fuselage
25ft 2in (7.67m)
Weight empty
4,620lb (2,097kg)
Weight loaded
6,100lb (2,769kg)
Cruising speed
110mph (177km/h)
Service ceiling
25,000ft (7,625m)
Hover ceiling IGE
22,000ft (6,170m)
Hover ceiling OGE
18,000ft (5,490m)
Range
303 miles (488km)

The 43F is primarily distinguished from the 'B' Huskie by a more powerful turbine engine. It is a particularly quiet helicopter which has established records for high availability and low accident rates.

One interesting aspect of the 'F' is its similarity to the QH-43G, which had, for five years, been performing classified missions for the U.S. Navy. The QH-43G (a drone helicopter) was set apart from the 'F' Huskie by its use as a high-altitude antenna support vehicle operating from the U.S.S. *Wright*.

U.S.A. Kamen /SH-2D Seasprite

Engine
Two (2) General Electric
T58-GE-8F ; 1,350shp
Rotor diameter
44ft 0in (13.41m)
Length overall
52ft 7in (16.03m)
Weight empty
6,953lb (3,153kg)
Weight loaded
12,800lb (5,805kg)
Cruising speed
150mph (241km/h)
Rate of climb
2,440ft/m (744m)
Service ceiling
22,500ft (6,858m)
Hover ceiling IGE
18,600ft (5,670m)
Hover ceiling OGE
15,400ft (4,695m)
Range
422 miles (679km)

This helicopter is unique
insofar as it is identified by a
U.S. Navy acronym : LAMPS
(Light Airborne Multi-Purpose
System), which calls for a
sophisticated package of
electronic and electromagnetic
sensors and weapons systems
for anti-submarine warfare and
anti-ship missile defence.

The SH-2D's LAMPS equip-
ment includes search radar,
electronic support measures,
magnetic anomaly detector,

marine markers, and a homing
torpedo. It also performs such
sea functions as search and
rescue, medical evacuation, surveillance, vertical replenishment
and communications relay.

U.S.A. Kamen /SH-2F Seasprite

Engine
Two (2) General Electric
T58-GE-8F; 1,350shp
Rotor diameter
44ft 0in (13.41m)
Length overall
52ft 7in (16.03m)
Weight empty
7,040lb (3,193kg)
Weight loaded
12,500lb (5,670kg)
Cruising speed
150mph (241km/h)
Rate of climb
2,440ft/m (744m)
Service ceiling
22,500ft (6,858m)
Hover ceiling IGE
18,600ft (5,670m)
Hover ceiling OGE
15,400ft (4,695m)
Range
422 miles (679km)

This newest configuration of the LAMPS helicopter programme has a '101' rotor, which eliminates vibrations and a new rotor control system of titanium assemblies which reduces the number of control elements by about 60 per cent.

The SH-2F has a stronger landing gear and improved radar and communications systems. A sensor operator joins the pilot and co-pilot. Space can be arranged to accommodate internal and external cargoes.

U.S.A. Piasecki /16H-3K Pathfinder III

Engine
Two (2) Pratt & Whitney
PT 6B-30; 750shp
Rotor diameter
44ft 2¾in (13.49m)
Length of fuselage
42ft 9½in (13.04m)
Weight empty
5,955lb (2,701kg)
Weight loaded
9,600lb (4,354kg)
Maximum speed
192mph (309km/h)
Range
850 miles (1,365km)

The Pathfinder is a high-speed aircraft designed to function as a VTOL (vertical take-off and landing), but can also carry large payloads in a STOL (short take-off and landing).

The model was originally planned as a commercial transport. Subsequent contracts from the military services resulted in transformation to a high-speed helicopter with improved power ratings. The Model III Pathfinder is being re-designed along similar lines as the II, but will be fitted with a four-bladed main rotor. It will also have an enlarged and improved cabin for marketing as an executive transport with accommodation for up to fifteen persons.

Engine
Lycoming IVO-360-A1A;
180hp
Rotor diameter
27ft 0in (8.23m)
Length overall
31ft 2in (9.50m)
Length of fuselage
24ft 1in (7.34m)
Weight empty
1,135lb (514kg)
Weight loaded
1,685lb (764kg)
Cruising speed
80mph (128km/h)
Rate of climb
1,200ft/m (366m)
Service ceiling
13,000ft (3,960m)
Hover ceiling IGE
7,300ft (2,225m)
Range
175 miles (280km)

A two-place utility helicopter, geared for training and patrol as well as sporting and recreational purposes.

The fuel-injected, vertically-mounted Lycoming engine drives the rotor through an automatic centrifugal clutch and multiple V-belt drive system. The main rotor gearbox has been eliminated to diminish noise and effect economy in maintenance.

The twin blades are mounted

in a patented 'Flexhub' system; the main rotor is of size to permit storage in a garage with an 8 x 9ft door.

Accessories include dual controls, lighting for night operations, ground-handling wheels, and auxiliary fuel tank.

Scheutzow is in process of launching two new sport helicopters (single place Hawk 90 and two-place Hawk 140) incorporating patented 'Bee' components.

U.S.A. Sikorsky /CH-3E

Engine
Two (2) General Electric
T58-GE-5 ; 1,500shp
Rotor diameter
62ft 0in (18.90m)
Length overall
73ft 0in (22.25m)
Length of fuselage
57ft 3in (17.45m)
Weight empty
13,255lb (6,010kg)
Weight loaded
22,050lb (10,000kg)
Cruising speed
144mph (232km/h)
Rate of climb
1,310ft/m (400m)
Service ceiling
11,000ft (3,385m)
Hover ceiling IGE
4,100ft (1,250m)
Range
465 miles (748km)

One of four variations of the
S-61R which the U.S. Air Force
chose in the early 1960s for
troop and cargo transportation.
It has a hydraulically-operated
ramp for rear loading, a
retractable landing gear, and
self-lubricating rotors. An
advanced weapons and
electronics system gives this
amphibious helicopter versatile-
mission potential.

U.S.A. Sikorsky/CH-53D

Engine
Two (2) General Electric
T64-GE-412; 3,695shp
Rotor diameter
72ft 3in (22.02m)
Length overall
88ft 3in (26.90m)
Length of fuselage
67ft 2in (20.47m)
Weight empty
23,485lb (10,653kg)
Weight loaded
36,400lb (16,510kg)
Cruising speed
173mph (278km/h)
Rate of climb
2,180ft/m (664m)
Service ceiling
21,000ft (6,400m)
Hover ceiling IGE
13,400ft (4,080m)
Hover ceiling OGE
6,500ft (1,980m)
Range
257 miles (413km)

The CH-53D is the U.S. Marine Corps improved version of the CH-53A. It has space arrangements for carrying up to 64 equipped troops. Most units of the helicopter possess special towing equipment for utilisation in mine-sweeping operations along harbours and beaches.

Its cargo-handling system can load and unload pallet-enclosed cargo at rate of one short ton per minute. The main and tail rotors are foldable for operation from aircraft carriers.

U.S.A. Sikorsky /CH-53E

Engine
Three (3) General Electric
T64-GE-415 ; 4,390shp
Rotor diameter
79ft 0in (24.08m)

Sikorsky is currently developing this three-engined turboshaft model, based on the CH-53D, in accordance with a U.S. Navy contract. The company's two prototypes (YCH-53E) were planned for initial flights in 1974, but production is now estimated for 1976 at the earliest.

The CH-53E is expected to have a transmission rated at 12,740shp. The craft will contain long-range fuel tanks, an all-weather navigation system, and an advanced automatic flight control system. It will be used for vertical replenishment and the removal of damaged aircraft from carrier craft. The U.S. Marine Corps envisions an airlift capable of removing 93 per cent of a division's combat items, and a 98 per cent retrieval of tactical aircraft without requiring disassembly.

Engine
Two (2) Pratt & Whitney
JFTD12-4A ; 4,000shp
Rotor diameter
72ft 0in (21.95m)
Length overall
88ft 6in (26.97m)
Length of fuselage
70ft 3in (21.41m)
Weight empty
19,234lb (8,724kg)
Weight loaded
42,000lb (19,050kg)
Cruising speed
105mph (169km/h)
Rate of climb
1,330ft/m (405m)
Service ceiling
9,000ft (2,475m)
Hover ceiling IGE
10,600ft (3,230m)
Hover ceiling OGE
6,900ft (2,100m)
Range
230 miles (370km)

This is the U.S. Army version of the original S-64 flying crane, designed for troop transport, cargo-movement, hospital service, and mine-sweeping operations.

The CH-54A's mission in the Vietnam war included the transportation of heavy hardware and vehicles, such as bulldozers and road-graders. In 1965, one helicopter lifted 90 people including 87 troops in a detachable van—considered a record lift.

Recent orders for the Skycrane have been placed by civilian concerns for oil drilling and exploration in Alaska and world-wide sites.

U.S.A. Sikorsky/HH-53B

The Sikorsky Model S-65A is a heavy assault transport helicopter produced in different versions for the U.S. Air Force, Navy and Marine Corps. The first variation was the CH-53A, which employed components of the Skycrane and has a hydraulically-operated cargo loading system.

The HH-53B is an U.S. Air Force helicopter designed for use (in 1967) by the Aerospace Rescue and Recovery Service. It has a retractable refuelling probe, two self-sealing fuel tanks, and a rescue hoist.

Engine
Two (2) General Electric T64-GE-3; 3,080shp
Rotor diameter
72ft 3in (22.02m)
Length overall
88ft 3in (26.90m)
Length of fuselage
67ft 2in (20.47m)
Weight empty
23,125lb (10,490kg)
Weight loaded
42,000lb (19,050kg)
Cruising speed
173mph (278km/h)
Rate of climb
1,440ft/m (440m)
Service ceiling
18,400ft (5,610m)
Hover ceiling IGE
8,100ft (2,470m)
Hover ceiling OGE
1,600ft (490m)
Range
540 miles (869km)

Engine
Two (2) General Electric
T64-GE-7; 3,435shp
Rotor diameter
72ft 3in (22.02m)
Length overall
88ft 3in (26.90m)
Length of fuselage
67ft 2in (20.47m)
Weight empty
23,569lb (10,690kg)
Weight loaded
42,000lb (19,050kg)
Cruising speed
173mph (278km/h)
Rate of climb
2,070ft/m (631m)
Service ceiling
20,400ft (6,220m)
Hover ceiling IGE
11,700ft (3,565m)
Hover ceiling OGE
4,300ft (1,310m)
Range
540 miles (869km)

An advanced version of the
HH-53B, the HH-53C is
powered by two turboshaft
engines of 3,435shp. Its rescue
hoist contains 250ft (76m) of
cable; the external cargo hook
possesses a 20,000lb (9,070kg)
capability.

U.S.A. Sikorsky /S-61A

Engine
Two (2) General Electric
T58-GE-10; 1,250shp
Rotor diameter
62ft 0in (18.90m)
Length overall
72ft 8in (22.15m)
Length of fuselage
54ft 9in (16.69m)
Weight empty
9,763lb (4,428kg)
Weight loaded
21,500lb (9,750kg)
Cruising speed
159mph (256km/h)
Rate of climb
1,500ft/m (457m)
Service ceiling
12,800ft (3,901m)
Range
541 miles (871km)

This twin-turbined amphibious transport is equipped to carry, in civil and military capacities, 12 passengers, 15 stretchers, or up to 26 troops. Rolls-Royce Bristol Gnome H-1200 turboshaft engines can be substituted for the General Electric power system. The Royal Danish Air Force operates a fleet of S-61As in its air-sea rescue activities.

U.S.A. Sikorsky /S-61 L

Engine
Two (2) General Electric
CT58-140-2 ; 1,500shp
Rotor diameter
62ft 0in (18.90m)
Length overall
72ft 10½in (22.21m)
Weight empty
11,701lb (5,308kg)
Weight loaded
19,000lb (8,620kg)
Cruising Speed
138mph (222km/h)
Rate of climb
1,300ft/m (395m)
Service ceiling
12,500ft (3,810m)
Hover ceiling IGE
9,000ft (2,743m)
Hover ceiling OGE
8,700ft (2,652m)
Range
265 miles (426km)

A commercial transport which (with the S-61N) became the first helicopter to obtain FAA approval for instrument flight operations.

The S-61L is non-amphibious. It has a non-retractable landing gear, pneumatic shock absorbers, a Goodyear tail wheel and Goodyear hydraulic disc brakes. It will accommodate up to 30 passengers.

In July 1972, New York Airways, covering metropolitan New York—one of the most crowded air traffic centres in the world—set a monthly record when it carried 40,858 passengers in its fleet of S-61L helicopters.

U.S.A. Sikorsky /S-61 N

Engine
Two (2) General Electric
CT58-140-2 ; 1,500shp
Rotor diameter
62ft 0in (18.90m)
Length overall
72ft 10in (22.20m)
Weight empty
12,336lb (5,595kg)
Weight loaded
10,000lb (4,540kg)
Cruising speed
138mph (222km/h)
Rate of climb
1,300ft/m (395m)
Service ceiling
12,500ft (3,810m)
Hover ceiling IGE
8,700ft (2,652m)
Hover ceiling OGE
3,800ft (1,158m)
Range
518 miles (833km)

The amphibious counterpart of
the S-61L, the S-61N has a
hydraulically-retractable landing
gear, but a non-retractable tail
wheel. Its all-metal fuselage is of
semi-monocoque structure.
Standard equipment includes
blind-flying instrumentation.
Rotor blades are not foldable.
   There are spaces for a crew
of three and accommodation
in the cabin for up to 28
passengers.

Engine
Pratt & Whitney PT6T-3 Twin
Pac; 1,600shp
Rotor diameter
56ft 0in (17.07m)
Length overall
65ft 10in (20.06m)
Length of fuselage
47ft 3in (14.4m)
Weight empty
7,400lb (3,356kg)
Weight loaded
13,000lb (5,896kg)
Cruising speed
127mph (204km/h)
Hover ceiling OGE
4,700ft (1,433m)
Range
299 miles (481km)

The piston-engined S-58 is now being converted to the twin-turbine S-58T, via kits, which the company is marketing as a helicopter with improved safety, reliability and performance at lower operating costs.

The rotor system comprises all-metal main and tail rotors with servo control. The main rotor blades are foldable. The landing gear is non-retractable with a three-wheel undercarriage and space for pontoons and flotation equipment.

The S-58T has side-by-side seats in the pilot's compartment and can accommodate up to 15 passengers in the cabin.

Adapted for the petroleum or construction industry, the S-58T can carry 16 passengers 300 miles (482km) or lift a 5,000lb (2,268kg) external load to 6,550ft (1,996m).

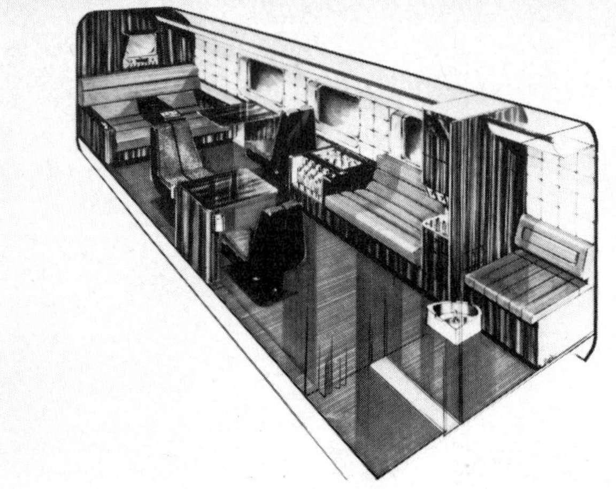

U.S.A. Sikorsky /S-67 Blackhawk

Engine
Two (2) General Electric
T58-GE-5 ; 1,500shp
Rotor diameter
62ft 0in (18.90m)
Length overall
74ft 4in (22.66m)
Length of fuselage
64ft 9in (19.74m)
Weight empty
12,514lb (5,676kg)
Weight loaded
22,050lb (10,002kg)
Cruising speed
187mph (301km/h)
Rate of climb
2,350ft/m (716m)
Service ceiling
17,000ft (5,180m)

Among the newest in the line of high-speed attack helicopters, the S-67 has a vertical fin, as in fixed-wing aircraft. A horizontal stabiliser is mounted in the rear of the fuselage and effects considerable reduction in vertical drag.

The S-67's armament includes TOW anti-tank missile pods, and turrets for 7.62mm guns, 30mm cannon and a 40mm grenade launcher.

In 1970 it set a world speed record at 220mph (355km/h) around a 15-mile (25km) course.

Engine
Two (2) General Electric
T58-GE-10 ; 1,400shp
Rotor diameter
62ft 0in (18.90m)
Length overall
72ft 8in (22.15m)
Length of fuselage
54ft 9in (16.69m)
Weight empty
11,865lb (5,382kg)
Weight loaded
18,626lb (8,449kg)
Cruising speed
136mph (219km/h)
Rate of climb
2,200ft/m (670m)
Service ceiling
14,700ft (4,480m)
Hover ceiling IGE
10,500ft (3,200m)
Hover ceiling OGE
8,200ft (2,500m)
Range
625 miles (1,005km)

This twin-turbine helicopter is one of many versions of Sikorsky's S-61 series of military and commercial helicopters.

The SH-3D Sea King has been the U.S. Navy's anti-submarine standard bearer since 1966, after which several were purchased by the Spanish and Brazilian navies. The helicopter has been licensed for production by Westland (U.K.), Agusta (Italy) and Mitsubishi (Japan).

The five-bladed main and tail rotors are all-metal ; the blades are interchangeable and foldable. Weapon capacity is 840lb (381kg). Electronic equipment includes Bendix sonar and Hamilton Standard autostabilisation equipment. Crew consists of pilot, co-pilot and two sonar operators.

U.S.A. Sikorsky /RH-53D

Engine
Two (2) General Electric
T64-GE-415; 7,560shp
Rotor diameter
72ft 3in (22.02m)
Length overall
88ft 3in (26.90m)
Length of fuselage
67ft 2in (20.47m)
Weight empty
22,444lb (10,180kg)
Weight loaded
50,000lb (22,680kg)
Ground turning radius
44ft 2in (13.46m)
Endurance
Over four (4) hours

This aircraft derives from the U.S. Navy's decision, in 1970, to establish helicopter mine counter-measures squadrons. Development was predicated on establishing an improved version of the CH-53, resulting in the designation, RH-53D.

Basic mission is to move equipment designed to sweep mechanical, acoustic and magnetic mines. The helicopter can also effect ship-to-helicopter refuelling while in the air, and is equipped with a filter to cut off the flow if impurities seep into the fuel. The helicopter is equipped with sophisticated towing equipment, storage racks, and magnetic and acoustical gear, in addition to having provisions for two 0.50 machine-guns used for detonating mines.

Engine
Two (2) General Electric
T700-GE-700 ; 1,500shp
Rotor diameter
53ft 0in (16.15m)
Weight loaded
15,850lb (7,189kg)

In 1972 Sikorsky and Boeing
Vertol were selected by the U.S.
Army to design, build and test
three prototype aircraft for its
Utility Tactical Transport
Aircraft System (UTTAS).

The Sikorsky model has two
advanced technology turbofan
engines and a four-bladed main
rotor. The fuselage is of semi-
monocoque light alloy ; the
landing gear is a non-retractable
tailwheel type, with a single
wheel on each unit to provide
protection for the tail rotor in
difficult terrain during taxying
and adverse landing conditions.
The helicopter will accommodate
a crew of three and eleven
troops. Four stretchers can be
substituted for eight troop seats
on medical evacuation missions.

The mock-up features a low
silhouette, large cockpit
windows to enlarge vision, and
large aft-sliding doors for
quick entry and exit of troops.

U.S.A. Sikorsky /S-70

The S-70 is the commercial
version of the UTTAS (Utility
Transport Aircraft System)—
the prototype of which is being
prepared for the U.S. Army.
Sikorsky plans to use its own
funds to build this helicopter,
which it considers to be particularly suitable for construction
and offshore oil applications.

U.S.S.R. Kamov /Ka-25K

Engines
Two (2) Glushenkov GTD-3;
900shp
Rotor diameter
51ft 8in (15.74m)
Length overall
32ft 3in (9.83m)
Weight empty
9,700lb (4,400kg)
Weight loaded
16,100lb (7,300kg)
Cruising speed
120mph (193km/h)
Service ceiling
11,500ft (3,500m)
Range
405 miles (650km)

A twin-turbine flying crane
helicopter, this is a commercial
counterpart of the Ka-25, an
anti-submarine helicopter which
has been allocated the NATO
code name, 'Hormone'.

The cabin of the Ka-25K can
accommodate twelve folding
seats for passengers. A
removable gondola provides
the pilot with a supervisory
position for cargo positioning
while the helicopter hovers.

The anti-submarine Ka-25
operates from carriers and
cruisers, and contains an
internal weapons-bay for stores
and torpedoes.

Dimensions of the Ka-25 and
Ka-25K are similar except that

the former has a slightly shorter
overall length 32ft (9.75m).

The Ka-25K rotor system
consists of two triple-blade
co-axial contra-rotating motors
with foldable blades. The tail unit
is all-metal; the landing gear a
non-retractable four-wheel
unit. Optional equipment
includes autopilot, radio
compass, and a day-night all-
weather lighting system.

A twin-engined light helicopter used extensively for agricultural missions in the dusting and spraying of orchards and vineyards. Passenger and cargo versions permit seating arrangements for up to seven passengers. The landing gear of the helicopter is fitted with floats that become inflatable from a special pneumatic system.

A ship-based version permits operation over water in searches for fish and ice patrols.

Transportation of bulky cargoes (up to 2,000lb; 900kg) are effected through general-purpose suspension sling, suspended from retaining lock controlled from the cockpit.

The Ka-26 is now operating in Rumania, Hungary, Bulgaria, East Germany, Sweden, West Germany, Mongolia, Yemen, Central African Republic, Sri-Lanka, and the U.S.A.

Engines
Two (2) M-14B26; 325hp
Rotor diameter
42ft 8in (13.00m)
Length of fuselage
25ft 5in (7.75m)
Weight empty
4,300lb (1,950kg)
Weight loaded
7,165lb (3,250kg)
Cruising speed
93mph (150km/h)
Service ceiling
9,840ft (3,000m)
Hover ceiling IGE
4,265ft (1,300m)
Hover ceiling OGE
2,625ft (800m)
Range
745 miles (1,200m)

U.S.S.R. Mil/Mi-6

Engines
Two (2) Soloviev D-25V
(TV-2BM) ; 5,500shp
Rotor diameter
114ft 10in (35.00m)
Length overall
136ft 11½in (41.74m)
Length of fuselage
108ft 10½in (33.18m)
Weight empty
60,055lb (27,240kg)
Weight loaded
93,700lb (42,500kg)
Cruising speed
155mph (250km/h)
Service ceiling
14,750ft (4,500m)
Range
900 miles (1,450km)

At one time the largest helicopter flying in the world, the turbo-driven twin-engined Mi-6 ; (which has the NATO code name, 'Hook') is produced in military and civilian versions. Its flying-crane role has been adapted for air-lifting drilling rigs to the Siberian oilfields, for transporting heavy construction materials, and the movement of men and equipment for the control of forest fires.

In a military capacity the Mi-6 can accommodate a crew of five and sixty-five troops with full field equipment. As an ambulance, it can be converted to transport forty-one stretcher cases and two medical attendants.

U.S.S.R. Mil /Mi-8

Engines
Two (2) Isotov TV-2-117A;
1,500shp
Rotor diameter
69ft 10¼in (21.29m)
Length overall
82ft 9¼in (25.24m)
Length of fuselage
60ft 0¼in (18.31m)
Weight loaded
26,400lb (12,000kg)
Cruising speed
140mph (225km/h)
Service ceiling
7,000ft (2,135m)
Hover ceiling IGE
6,233ft (1,800m)
Hover ceiling OGE
2,625ft (800m)
Range
750 miles (1,200km)

A multi-purpose helicopter available in passenger and transport versions. The fuselage is an all-metal semi-monocoque. The nose portion accommodates a cockpit designed for two pilots and a flight engineer. The undercarriage is a non-retracting tricycle with gas-oil shock absorbers. The two-stage epicyclic main gearbox drives the tail rotor, a fan, hydraulic pumps, and an alternator. There is one standby drive.

The main rotor is five-bladed with a three-hinge hub. The

blades are all-metal, with aluminium-alloy pressed spars and honeycomb trailing edge sections. The fully-powered flight controls incorporate single-action control boosters which operate from a duplicated hydraulic system.

The passenger version can seat up to thirty-two persons. The seats can be removed for conversion as a cargo transport. A system can be provided for external suspension of cargoes up to 3,000kg (6,600lb), and a winch with an airborne jib which permits loading of cargoes of up to 200kg (440lb) in the hover. Ambulance conversion takes twelve stretchers and an attendant.

U.S.S.R. Mil/Mi-10

Engines
Two (2) Soloviev D-25V;
5,500hp
Rotor diameter
114ft 10in (35.00m)
Length overall
137ft 5½in (41.89m)
Length of fuselage
107ft 9¾in (32.86m)
Weight empty
60,185lb (27,300kg)
Weight loaded
96,340lb (43,700kg)
Cruising speed
112mph (180km/h)
Service ceiling
9,850ft (3,000m)
Range
155 miles (250km)

This flying crane was based on the Mi-6 helicopter and intended expressly for transportation of bulky cargoes slung externally. Among the interchangeable units of the Mi-6 are the main and tail rotors, power plant and transmission, hydraulic systems, control system, equipment and de-icing system. Small-size cargoes can be carried in the cargo cabin inside the fuselage. An auxiliary power unit ensures operation of the helicopter in field conditions.

The undercarriage is of four-strut design with gas-oil shock-

absorbers. The cargo platform is all-metal and fitted with four supports, ramps, cargo-attachment units and three wheels for ground transportation. The main rotor hub is of five-bladed, three-hinge construction, with hydraulic dampers. The tail rotor is four-bladed, with feathering hinges. The main gearbox drives a fan, alternator and hydraulic system pumps. Control of the helicopter is maintained with the aid of control boosters operating from duplicated hydraulic systems.

The Mi-10 accommodates a crew of three, and has twenty-eight foldable seats. An American concern, Petroleum Helicopters, has purchased one craft for its oil-rig activity.

Engines
Two (2) Soloviev D-25V;
5,500shp
Rotor diameter
114ft 10in (35.00m)
Length overall
137ft 5½in (41.89m)
Length of fuselage
107ft 9¾in (32.86m)
Weight empty
54,410lb (24,680kg)
Weight loaded
83,776lb (38,000kg)
Cruising speed
155mph (250km/h)
Service ceiling
9,850ft (3,000m)
Range
494 miles (795km)

The Mi-10K, based on the design of the Mi-10, is operated as a flying crane with externally slung loads. Unlike the Mi-10, it has a low four-wheel under-carriage whose reduced weight permits a 3-ton increase in payload. The cabin can accommodate small-size cargoes and up to twenty-eight passengers in folded seats.

The helicopter is fitted with a four-channel autopilot to ensure flight stabilisation. With engagement of the autopilot, override is always possible and the pilot can take over at any time.

Engines
Four (4) Soloviev D-25VF;
6,500shp
Rotor diameter
114ft 10in (35.00m)
Length of fuselage
121ft 4½in (37.00m)
Weight empty
55,000lb (25,000kg)
Weight loaded
231,000lb (105,000kg)
Cruising speed
150mph (240km/h)
Service ceiling
11,500ft (3,500m)
Range
310 miles (500km)

A heavy-duty, multi-purpose
helicopter which, in 1969,
received acclaim for lifting
maximum loads to record
heights. On one occasion, the
helicopter, with a crew of six,
lifted 88,636lb (40,205kg) to
7,398ft (2,255m).

The four turboshaft engines
of the Mi-12 are mounted
side-by-side under fixed wings;
each pair to drive a rotor. The
rotors are cross-shafted for
maintenance of rotation in the
event of engine failure. The
fuselage is all-metal, semi-
monocoque construction. The
landing gear is a non-retracting
tricycle, with twin wheels on
each unit.

The Mi-12 can accommodate
a crew of six and provide
foldable seats for fifty troops or
work personnel.

The NATO code for the
Mi-12 is 'Homer'. Aeroflot
operates the helicopter in its
civil capacity as a support craft
for movement of freight,
geophysical survey equipment,
and to serve oil and natural gas
exploration in remote areas.

West Germany Technik München Sky-Trac 1

A two-seat multi-purpose light helicopter which Helikopter Technik München put into production in 1969 as a torque-free aircraft capable of serving diverse functions (cargo, ambulance, agricultural) with certain specialised equipment.

The rotor system includes two unfoldable blades of light alloy and a fitted rotor brake. The landing gear possesses pontoons for amphibious operations. Fuel capacity is 59 imperial gallons (270 litres).

The Sky-Trac can be enlarged by two additional spaces for passenger duty through provision of special kit materials.

Engine
Franklin 6AS-335-B; 260hp
Rotor diameter
34ft 1½in (10.40m)
Length overall
34ft 1in (10.40m)
Length of fuselage
24ft 1¼in (7.35m)
Weight empty
1,930lb (875kg)
Weight loaded
3,306lb (1,500kg)
Cruising speed
87mph (140km/h)
Rate of climb
1,180ft/m (360m)
Service ceiling
12,665ft (3,860m)
Range
348 miles (560km)

Technik München Skyrider

Engine
Franklin 6AS-335-B ; 260hp
Rotor diameter
34ft 1½in (10.40m)
Length overall
34ft 1½in (10.40m)
Length of fuselage
24ft 4½in (7.43m)
Weight loaded
3,306lb (1,500kg)
Cruising speed
106mph (170km/h)
Rate of climb
394ft/m (120m)
Service ceiling
12,665ft (3,860m)
Hover ceiling IGE
5,800ft (1,770m)
Hover ceiling OGE
5,000ft (1,525m)
Range
422 miles (680km)

The Skyrider, as unveiled in 1973, is similar to the Sky-Trac but with modification kit for conversion to a four-seater. It has, in addition, a glass-fibre cabin with fairings and an engine-driven alternator to furnish electric power. The air-conditioning system and a cargo sling are optional.

West Germany Messerschmitt-Bolkow-Blohm BO 105 C

This is a twin-engine multi-purpose helicopter, employing a hingeless, four-bladed main rotor and a two-bladed tail rotor with titanium anti-erosion strips. The fuselage is of lightweight semi-monococque aluminum construction. The engine is an internal combustion turboshaft.

Exclusive sales rights for the Western hemisphere have been allocated to Boeing Vertol by MBB which, through a 1969 amalgamation of Messerschmitt-Bolkow and Hamburger Flugzeugbau, has become Germany's largest aerospace employer (ca. 20,000 employees).

Engines
Two (2) Allison 250-C20; derated to 317shp
Rotor diameter
32ft 2¾in (9.82m)
Length overall
38ft 10in (11.84m)
Length of fuselage
28ft 0½in (8.55m)
Weight empty
2,447lb (1,110kg)
Weight loaded
5,070lb (2,300kg)
Cruising speed
144mph (232km/h)
Rate of climb
1,870ft/m (570m)
Service ceiling
16,500ft (5,030m)
Hover ceiling IGE
8,900ft (2,720m)
Range
360 miles (575km)

West Germany VFW-Fokker CH-53G

Engines
Two (2) General Electric
T64-GE-7; 3,230shp
Rotor diameter
72ft 3in (22.00m)
Length of fuselage
67ft 2in (20.50m)
Weight empty
24,000lb (10,950kg)
Weight loaded
42,000lb (19,051kg)
Cruising speed
175mph (278km/h)
Rate of climb
2,360ft/m (720m)
Hover ceiling IGE
10,570ft (3,222m)
Hover ceiling OGE
4,860ft (1,480m)
Range
190 miles (300km)

A co-production agreement between VFW-Fokker, of West Germany, and the U.S.A.'s Sikorsky Aircraft resulted in agreement to produce 110 each of the American's Model CH-53G under the former's management. Delivery, which began at the end of 1971, was planned for completion in 1975.

The turbo-engined CH-53G's capability of transporting thirty-eight fully equipped soldiers makes it one of the largest craft of its kind in the world. The airframe is aluminum-alloy; components in the vicinity of the rotor head, engine mounting and fireproof bulkhead are of titanium or steel. The fuselage, which is divided into five sections for production reasons, is of monococque construction with frames, longerons and skin fairings.

The helicopter's electrical power is supplied by two 3-phase AC generators which supply the electrical systems with 28V DC and AC current. (The generators are driven by the main transmission system via the auxiliary gearbox.)

Conversion can be effected for first-aid missions (24 stretchers; 4 attendants) and cargo duty (external loads on hooks up to 20,000lb (9,070kg)).